SALESFREAK

SALESFREAK

How To Become A Sales Rockstar By Finding a Killer Value Proposition in Every Sales Opportunity.

By

PRASHANT DONGRE

*This book is dedicated
to the salesperson within all of us!*

What's in it for you?

You will learn-

1. How to **sell** more
2. How to have a successful sales **career**
3. How to link 1 and 2

The PURPOSE of writing this book

Engineers, doctors, and finance professionals start to learn about their profession in schools and universities. Salespeople do not have that luxury!

Most people in sales do not receive any formal coaching to build the competencies they require to be the best in their roles. People learn from their colleagues and some hard experiences while they are on the job.

Our education does not focus so much on developing sales and marketing skills the way it focuses on developing technical and analytical skills.

I have been in sales for the last 20 years, and this is

the only job I ever had so far! After completing my degree in Chemical Engineering, I started in sales, not because I had a passion for selling, but because that was just the job I took to make a living! While working, I also studied Business Management for two years, only to realize that it does not offer much real-life selling guidance.

However, over time, I started liking the nature of my work as a salesperson, and today, I think this is the only work I want to do for the rest of my working life.

Who is it for?

1. For salespeople, this book will show you how to find a killer **value proposition** in every potential sale and present it to your customer. The book will bring a fresh **perspective** on various aspects of selling. You will be able to sell more.
2. For sales leaders, the book will help you have a better **impact** on your organization's revenue, processes, and culture.
3. It also addresses the elephant in the room-YOU! It will create an awareness in you to make good choices in your **career**, challenge yourself, and improve your visibility to your customers.

   You will sell more and have **growth opportunities,** including leadership roles, which are also discussed in the book.

What type of selling is discussed in this book?

This book is aimed at businesses that are selling products, technologies, projects, and solutions that are not yet commoditized. The focus of the book is **business to business (B2B),** i.e., selling that involves multiple stakeholders, face to face interactions, and many gray areas when it comes to decision-making.

"Complex sales" is where your typical clients are government and big corporations, and prices range from a few hundred thousand dollars to millions of dollars per transaction. These sales are difficult by nature, but they are also where the most **money** can be made.

The recurring theme of this book is to sell your products and services at good **profit** margins by offering **critical insights** into the value proposition to the customers. Being profitable is the only way to **sustain** your business in the longer run.

I hope that you will find this book useful and actionable. I will be delighted to receive your feedback at iprad21@gmail.com.

Happy selling!

1st May 2020

Contents

PART I:

BUILD THE FOUNDATION

Get yourself in order!

I

Should You Be Selling?

Now that you have bought this book, is this not a weird question to begin?

In the 21st century, we are all trying to put our ideas into each other's minds and get what we need or want. Irrespective of the nature of your work, you are always selling something to someone all the time. Other people are also selling something to you all the time, which, essentially, means that we are all salespeople, even if we do not have the title.

High-speed internet, social media revolution, and the ease of being visible to potential customers are bringing practically unlimited opportunities to start your own business or work for someone and make money.

Most sales jobs have some challenges and rewards.

Here are the typical **Challenges** in the sales job-

1. Travel

Depending on what you sell and where the clients are located, you will be required to travel, meaning time away from the family. Willingness to travel is directly linked to how well you will do in the job.

If your business requires you to travel long-distance across the continents, you will spend a lot of your time on flights and in airport lounges. Your mobile will remember lots of wi-fi passwords!

Traveling could be fun in the initial days of your career, but over time, you have a family and kids, and things are not always that rosy. You must like what you do to continue traveling for the most part of the career.

2. Targets

Business in general, and sales in particular, is a numbers game. All your ideas, resources, and efforts are aimed at one and one thing only- to make more money for your company. There will always be an expectation to bring in more business. Of course, this translates into more financial growth for you if you are excellent at your job.

Are you the type of person who likes goals set yearly? You will be expected to achieve or exceed them every year. And after you achieve them by the end of the year, the next year starts when the clock resets to zero, and you begin all over again! This will continue as long as you work.

3. Uncertainty

Predicting how clients will decide is hard. Predicting how markets will behave is much harder and totally beyond your control. There will always be things you simply don't know, and you will be dealing with many unknowns throughout your sales career yet still be expected to achieve results! Isn't that challenging?

You will make a lot of decisions based on whatever information you have on hand and make many assumptions. You will continuously juggle facts, opinions, and feelings!

Many things will be urgent! This is a job where things just land at your desk unanticipated. It could still be a 9 to 5 job, but you will have challenges and many decisions to make throughout your career.

4. Some angry clients

No matter how polite and customer-focused you are, there will be some angry clients. No matter which department in your organization screws up, it is you who will take the flak! And no matter how angry you get, you will be required to keep a smiling face and salvage the situation. After all, you want to revisit the same client and get more business.

Customer satisfaction is an interesting topic, and continual effort is needed to keep your customers satisfied.

Don't feel depressed after reading the above points as there is also a bright side to a career in sales. There is no such thing as gain without pain, and the same is true in this career. For all the challenges that you overcome and sacrifices you and your family make, here are the **rewards**!

Rewards-

The job could also bring some or all the below

rewards-

1. It's a good sport!

By its very nature, sales is a competitive sport. In every transaction, you will either win or lose. If you win, you learn somethings that works. If you lose, there is always another chance to win the next one!

2. Satisfaction

There is tremendous joy and satisfaction to be achieved from a happy customer who wants to do more business with you. You have built a lot of trust with this client, and a long-term business relationship has been forged.

Realizing a sale is like a jigsaw puzzle game. You must find all or most of the critical pieces and then join them together.

3. Traveling the world

I have been lucky to work for companies and businesses that required me to travel to more than 15 countries in the last 20 years and do business with so many nationalities. This has helped me grow personally and learn a lot of new things about different cultures.

You start appreciating that we are all the same despite different cultures. You also start to be humble, which is essential for continuous learning in your career and life.

Meeting people of different cultures can be a great learning experience in the long run. Moreover, interacting with people who do not necessarily agree with you or challenge your ideas from time to time can help you get a unique perspective about life and can fuel your personal growth.

4. Great Career opportunities

Being in sales requires you to be up close to the market. If you are doing it well, a company will appreciate your value as a potential employee because of the information and knowledge you bring to the table. This translates into exciting career opportunities for you.

If you want to start a small business, you will know where to focus from the beginning!

So, whether you wish to work for someone or have ambitions to start your own business, having spent a few years in sales will boost your chances of having a meaningful and successful career.

This does not mean that you must enjoy all the aspects of your work to make sales. Sales could be a stepping stone for you to springboard your career into different areas.

One of the good things about sales is that it can accelerate you up the hierarchy without giving you gray hair. Very few other parts of the business accelerate you up the tree as fast. This is because you can prove your value through your numbers. It is meritocratic – not just tenure.

5. Purpose

Lack of purpose is one of the most significant factors contributing to the lack of employee engagement at work. During the early part of my career, I was in this boat, and life was not that exciting.

Because you meet so many people and solve their problems with your products and services, it can help you to find purpose in your work. While this sounds philosophical, finding a purpose can take you on a path of extraordinary achievement and a sense of accomplishment that very few people are able to achieve.

If you have a sense of purpose that you bring to your sales job every day, you will have enough ideas and strength to overcome problems that will always arise due to the nature of this job. In fact, you will develop qualities that many people lack in the workplace, and this will have a tremendous positive impact on your career.

So, even if you are currently in sales, be sure to take a step back and ask yourself if you want to be selling as a full-time job for the rest of your life. Keeping in mind some of the above challenges and rewards, I suggest you take some time to think about the below questions to know if this is the right career choice for you. Do online research and consult people you know about having a sales career.

If you have thought this through and have concluded that sales is the next or only job you want to do, then you must start understanding and mastering the different aspects of this job to become the best in this game.

Your goal is not to become just a salesperson. It is to become the best version of yourself in a sales job and make a positive difference in your career and society. This book will show you exactly how to do both.

QUESTIONS FOR LEARNING

1. Which are my three long-term career goals?
2. Which short-term goals do I need to aim for to meet the long-term goals?
3. Will a career in sales help me achieve these goals? How?
4. What assumptions am I making that must be proven correct?

NEXT STEP

We will discuss the career aspects of a sales job and how to find the right balance. We will delve into the anticipated future of what will affect the way we sell.

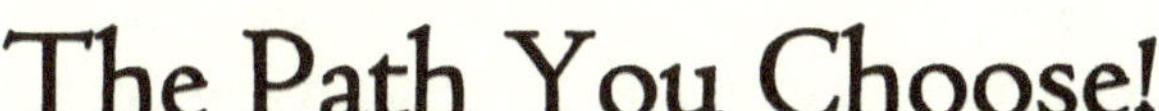

The Path You Choose!

Whether selling or working for someone else or have your own business, you will spend 40 or more years of your life working! That is plenty of time, and it calls for some serious consideration toward which career you choose and what factors affect your choice for today and tomorrow.

Before we start, let us get one myth out of the way. Career growth does not necessarily mean only growing up, i.e., vertical. It could also be lateral, where one can take on different responsibilities at the same level without climbing up the career ladder.

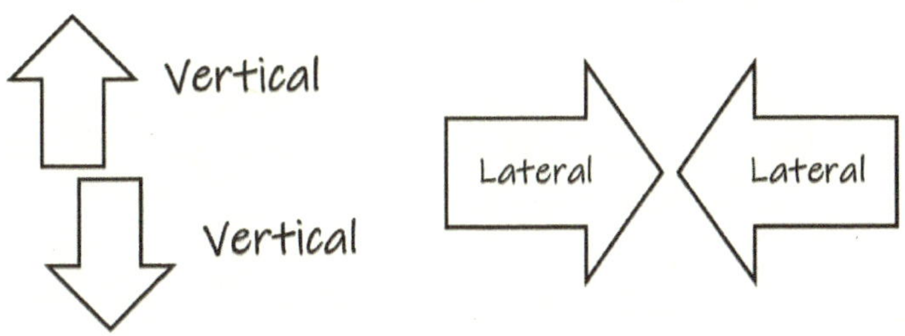

When starting your career at a trainee level, you will have a high probability of moving up. So, you will surely have a vertical growth for some time. When you reach a certain level of competence and experience, things can start looking different. From now on, moving up is not the only choice you have!

With experience, you could decide to pursue other areas in your business, and hence, move laterally in your career. This could also help you establish a solid base and be great at obtaining more than one area of expertise.

For example, you could be selling one product for 5-10 years and have developed expertise in it. As a lateral move, you could start selling some other product or technology in the same company.

Also, you could be in a leadership role and might not like it! In that case, you could try some other position where you have no one reporting to you, and you are all by yourself.

As companies get leaner, the chances of vertical growth also get fewer, and you will always have to think and decide for yourself which direction you wish to go!

It all boils down to how good you know yourself and how realistic your expectations are.

Whether you choose to take vertical or lateral path, there are some key factors that affect your career.

Let's discuss them one by one-

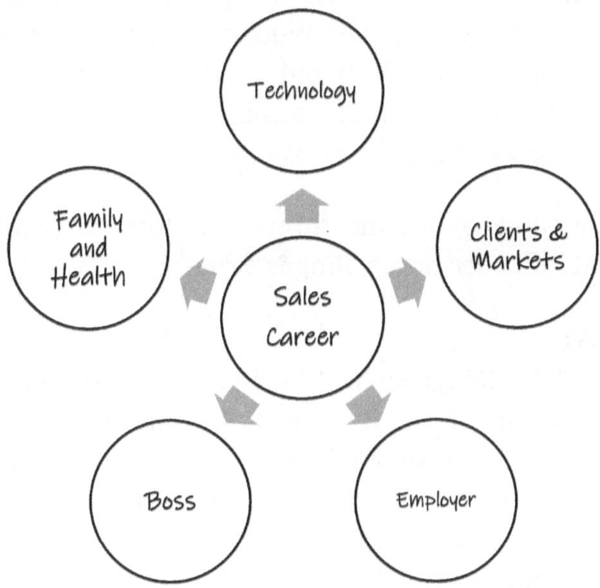

1. Technology

Things always change!

Technology drives our daily lives and has a significant impact on how to conduct business.

Let's take the speed of doing business as an example. Before the internet era, the primary modes of communication in sales were the telephone, courier, and fax. In today's context, things were very slow, and it would take days for any sales to complete.

This was also reflected in the expectations the customers had from their suppliers.

Things have changed with the accessibility of the internet. Today, business is done at the speed of light! Things are fast and much more effective, giving lots of options to sellers and buyers. The information is freely available and consumed quickly to form impressions and make decisions.

If we think about the future, the following things could influence how selling is done-

- **AI**

Artificial intelligence will likely take a quantum leap and be involved in many buying and selling processes. Because of advanced algorithms, objective decision-making will be the norm of future buyers. That means salespeople will become more and more acquainted with AI and how to use it to sell effectively. We are already on this path, and if you have a Customer Management System (CRM) like Salesforce, you will understand how!

There is no avoiding an AI-based future, which means every salesperson who wants to have a career in sales and a job will have to figure out how to use it.

- **Social Media**

Social media will play a key role in how your products, services, and you as a salesperson are perceived by your clients. Corporate branding and sales promotion of the future will look vastly different than it does today. With the costs of social media promotion going down to almost free, almost every small, medium, and big business will use it more and more, and that will have a tremendous impact on the sales process.

Social media will also spawn many careers for salespeople as freelancers. Finding the customers will become easier, and one will no longer need to work for some corporation to earn a decent living. If you are creative and offer something that people find useful, you will have a great shot at making it big. This has not been possible during most of human history. We live in a golden age of creativity and accessibility.

- **Value-based selling**

Anything that can be commoditized will be bought and sold via online platforms and won't require salespeople. Think about how much one can buy from Amazon today without the need to go to any shops.

This means value-based selling is the only way to survive and thrive if you do it well.

- **Fewer Hierarchies**

With so many disruptions, companies will hire fewer salespeople resulting in the reduction of corporate hierarchies.

This also means there will be not many managers in your company, and you could be managing yourself to a large extent using the many new tools available for you to excel in your job.

• **Multiple careers**

Today, most people work in one or two industries all their lives. But with AI disrupting so many industries in the future, it is unlikely that you will work in the same industry all your life. Many existing industries and markets will go extinct, and many new ones will appear, giving tremendous opportunities for sales careers and employment in general. This is a good thing as it will foster continuous learning and collaboration.

• **Finding Purpose**

A hundred years ago, most people were financially poor with a lower life expectancy. Most people used to work only for money to feed their families, and a career was something that used to happen as they spent their lifetime in the same company. Modern concepts like well-being at work were unthinkable!

Advances in science and technology have made our world more prosperous and a lot better place today. The future is going to be awesome, and most of humanity will live a good quality, long and healthy life!

What does this have to do with a sales job?

Well, the focus is already shifting from working to just earn money toward working for a purpose. This has far-reaching consequences for people management and corporate culture. The successful salespeople of the future will be the ones who have a definite purpose and know what they want out of their sales job apart from just money.

Aside from AI, the search for purpose in daily work will define how we work in a significant part of the 21st century!

So why are we discussing so much future? The fact is that the future has almost arrived! We are all in transition, and the speed of this transition is different in different industries and businesses.

You must be able to effectively combine what you know today about your job and what your perception is about the future of your job. And your perception of the future should be based on some hard data, objective thinking, and being humble about where you stand in this flux!

Technology will continue to shape and disrupt your future as a salesperson.

2. Clients and markets

Your career depends a lot on how proactive you are but also on the market in which you operate and the clients you serve. If you work in markets that are stagnant and have a low barrier to entry for new players, you will have a hard time selling, no matter how good you are at it.

The key to success in any market is to be proactive and resilient. Sometimes it can be hard to accept, but taking correct actions is the only thing one can do to sell more. Just like most things in life, markets go up and down, and before you know it, the dark clouds are gone, and your efforts start showing stellar results.

3. Your company

Assuming you are competent to do your job, and you operate in a big and lucrative market, the company you work for still impacts your career. When deciding to pursue a career with your company, always look at its culture and how ambitious and practical your leadership team is for growing the business in a sustainable way.

Also, find out how good your company is in terms of compliance and doing business ethically. It is essential that your values are aligned.

4. Your Manager

Your manager has a direct impact on your growth or the lack of it! It is understood that you don't get to choose your manager, but you could do a lot after you get one!

It is critical to understand what your manager is

looking for in your role as a salesperson and a team member. If you are not clear, consider having a direct talk. It is your responsibility to make sure that you and your manager are aligned for short and long-term goals that you as a team wish to pursue. Set up 1:1 meetings every 15 days with your manager and discuss the expectations as well as your progress. Seek and give feedback. Over time, you will have a better alignment.

Assuming your manager is also ambitious, do they give you a chance to grow vertically or laterally? This is an excellent question to ask yourself. There are a few parameters that can help you gauge it.

- How much your manager trusts you?
- Do they delegate important jobs to you? Do they delegate at all?
- Are they often telling you what to do?

5. Family and health

Since you are in sales, the chances are you travel frequently. This means time away from your family and eating outside on a regular basis. Your career is impacted if your family and health are not well.

Make a conscious effort to balance work and life and seek support from your manager if you find it is affecting your job. There is no shame in doing this, rather, it will show that you trust your manager to help you find a solution.

Your career growth, or the lack of it, is your responsibility. Do not outsource it to your manager. Just tell yourself that your managers and leaders are busy figuring out their own next career moves.

Before we jump to actual selling, reflect upon these aspects of your career.

QUESTIONS FOR LEARNING

1. Which is a better sales career path for me right now- vertical or lateral? Why?
2. Which lateral career opportunities are available for me?
3. Which technological trends are affecting my career most? How do I adapt to them?

NEXT STEP

Sales is a dynamic job. To keep you grounded and have a chance to succeed, you need to get one important thing right.

Integrity.

Let's talk about it.

3

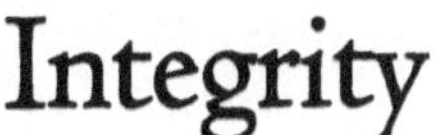

Integrity

You can go only so far with talent and hard work. But when you combine integrity with talent and hard work, you can reach a whole new level of success. Integrity is something that you cannot do without.

What is integrity, anyway?

Integrity is doing the right things 100% of the time. Integrity is doing your work even if nobody is watching. Integrity is finding your values and sticking to them all the time. No exceptions!

How do you know you have integrity?

If others, including your superiors, trust you with crucial responsibilities, this is a clear sign of your competence and dependability. It could also be the sign that they know that you have integrity, and hence, you are trustworthy.

On the other hand, if you make false promises to your customers or lie to them, that is going to be detrimental to you and your company.

If you find yourself sometimes (or continuously) thinking about ways to shirk work or take sick leave when you are fit, you probably need to do some root cause analysis.

If you blame others for your mistakes, you clearly lack a sense of ownership. If you take credit for other people's work, your peers most likely know this, and hence, they don't consider you trustworthy, let alone a team player.

If you spread rumors or negativity about your colleagues, managers, or certain situations in the office, consider that others will know this soon and form a negative impression of you, which will be almost impossible to change.

What to do if you find out you don't have integrity at the level it is required? Can this trait be developed?

If you find yourself doing some of the negative things mentioned above, you probably lack the integrity required to be in the job, let alone be excellent at it.

It is a myth that integrity is something you have or don't. Just like most skills, you can develop integrity with conscious effort. But unlike most skills that can be developed by learning and practicing, this one will require you to understand yourself better and make a commitment to change if needed. This is the tricky part because this change needs to be from inside. You must be disciplined and have a desire to get better.

Below are a few ways you can do it-

1. Values

Your values are your beliefs based on your perception of the world around you. They tell you what is right and what is wrong from your point of view. They are a combination of your upbringing, your aspirations, and how you go about achieving your goals. Think hard about which values are useful and which ones you need to adjust or discard. Find a mentor, friend, or colleague to talk to about them. Once you conclude what you need to change, change it.

2. Actions

Actions and motivation go hand in hand. Motivation leads to actions, and actions lead to motivation. You act because you have some motivation, and you create motivation by actions. The important thing here is the right actions. How do you define the right actions? Well, that's why you have goals. Apart from goals that are linked to your business, take actions that are aligned to your values.

Whenever you are unsure of what to do, put your company first. Do the right thing in the first place rather than doing things right afterward.

3. Find peers with integrity

Rather than just visualizing people with high integrity, find people in your company who are smarter than you and have a lot of integrity. Associate with them, and it soon becomes impossible to associate with cynical and lazy people. You just set your benchmark high by following smart people and copying them if necessary. When you do it consistently, you will drastically make yourself more valuable to your company.

4. Make commitments

To prevent you from not keeping your promises, make written commitments. Write to a client that you will visit them next week and leave yourself very little room not to show up. Tell your boss that you will improve a specific skill and will make a short presentation in the next three months. When the stakes are high, it will be difficult to bail out. This way, you create a habit of doing what you have committed.

Over time, this habit helps you get a reputation as dependable, and before you know it, people start looking at you as someone with integrity.

If you are in a sales leadership role, spend a good amount of time before you recruit the next salesperson. Check the candidate's background, ask them to demonstrate their teamwork and integrity apart from their contacts and sales numbers.

QUESTIONS FOR LEARNING

1. What are my values? Which ones are not aligned with my business and vice versa? What could I do to get them aligned?
2. Which type of people do I surround myself with?
3. What actions should I set to develop integrity? Whom shall I look up to?

NEXT STEP

Now that we have laid the foundation, let's talk about why you are hired in the first place and how to exceed the expectations of your employer consistently.

PART II:

GAIN MOMENTUM

Learn sales fundamentals!

4

Hired For What?

The primary objective of any business is simple—spend as little money as possible and make as much money as possible. You have been hired to solve specific problems in a superior way than other market players. Your employer expects you to sell your product or service and make **maximum profit** for your company. As you are reading this book, you want to become a damn good salesperson and are willing to go the extra mile to sell more.

Business is a game of perceptions. Once your product quality is at par with your competitors, salespeople and their selling methods are the main differentiating tools that can give an edge to your company over the others.

Just because you are in sales or business development does not mean you know the full spectrum of your tasks and job responsibilities.

While it might seem unnecessary, you must invest a good deal of time and energy to figure out what you have been hired to do? Only after you understand your role clearly, can you think about excelling in that role. Once you have this clarity, every sale you do, every meeting you attend with the client, will become a stepping stone toward making you a highly effective salesperson. This will help your organization grow its business and will help you climb the corporate ladder if this is your career goal. If you don't aspire to be in a leadership role, being an effective salesperson will prove valuable in absolutely any endeavor you undertake in your career.

You will become valuable in the market you serve because your customers know that you solve their problems!

Willingness to improve will also teach you humility. If you lack in some areas, you will be able to accept it and act to improve the weaknesses. This is the only way to improve. Many salespeople are not humble enough to acknowledge that they have some areas for improvement, and hence, never improve and remain mediocre.

Being clear about what you have been hired to do will give you the freedom to stop doing things you are not supposed to do. This can be very liberating and will contribute to your results.

Depending on the industry or sector you work in, you

should be aware of some or all the below areas that affect your daily job as a salesperson-

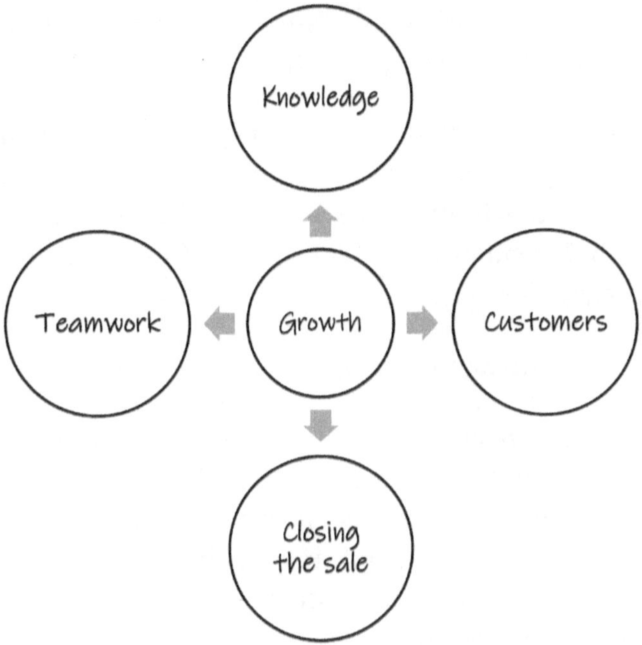

1. Product and service knowledge

For you to understand your client's requirements, it is imperative to know what products and services you offer as well as don't offer. You must be competent and excel at communicating with your clients.

Once you know what you offer, this will help you ask probing questions of your clients and get more information, so you build your value proposition more effectively. You will be more confident and agile, and your customers will start trusting you more, giving you more business.

While it seems obvious, many salespeople don't fully know what their company offers!

Having said that, don't obsess with product knowledge. There is such thing as overkill – you know so much that you want to tell the customer too much. It's super important to keep things simple for the customer.

2. Customer meetings

You are responsible for meeting your clients regularly and building a long-term relationship with them. Customers have a short memory, and hence, you must show up from time to time, so they don't forget you. Your competition is knocking at their doors more often than you think!

When your clients have problems with your or competitor's product, you want to be the first person to get a call from them. This is where a good relationship with your client will help you. This will put you in a pole position when you start solving the problem compared to your competition. You simply get more time to solve the problem.

When it comes to the competition, every potential sale is a zero-sum game! You and your competitors operate in the same market. You are mostly fighting for the same piece of the pie, and if you lose, the other wins.

Gathering market intelligence is a key part of your work. As you go to clients, you are your company's eyes and ears to know what is happening in the market. It is also important that you inform your customer about the market. The customer is always trying to evaluate what the difference is between you and your competitors. You must be up to date on this point and must communicate clearly.

This is also why you need to travel and meet different clients regularly. Sitting in front of your desk is the worst strategy to figure out what is happening in the market! Even the internet has limited information available on market intelligence. It is your prime duty to collect as much correct information as you can and make good use of it.

Last but not least, for every customer visit, it is important to dress professionally. Your clothing need not be expensive, but it should help you build credibility with the customer. Your company is charging its customers a lot of money for their product, and therefore, you should look like the one worthy of it.

3. Closing the sale

After doing all it takes to hook your client on your products and services, your job must involve closing the sale. Depending on the sale, you could be doing this by yourself or with your bosses. But this is a vital part of your role, and you must learn to excel in this at all costs. Try not to give anything away for free. Negotiation is a series of transactions.

Communicate with your potential clients in easy and understandable ways. Use the right combination of phone calls, emails, and face to face meetings. This combination will vary depending on business and type of persons. In general, priority should be given to face to face meetings followed by phone calls. Emails should be the result of a discussion or a meeting rather than the main communication channel.

The idea here is to show to the client that you want to close the sale without being seen as pushy or desperate. Don't make too many phone calls. If you are approaching the decision-maker, make sure that you convey your message simply and clearly.

If you have closed the sale, are you done? No!

You also have to make sure that the client pays 100% of the agreed amount.

Let me share a short story. I was in my final year of engineering when I appeared for my 1st ever interview. It was for a sales job. The interviewer explained what they did and asked me what I thought my job should be. With zero experience, I had nothing to lose, so I shot a few obvious answers! He kept asking what else a few times until he realized I couldn't come up with anything more.

He smiled and asked if I didn't want to collect the money from the customer for the sale I had done? I will never forget that part of the interview. Still, I was hired, and that's where my journey as a salesperson started!

4. Teamwork

Your customers are important, and the success of your job depends on how you serve them.

But nobody makes it alone; you must have colleagues, bosses, and experts in your organization supporting you to win business. Teamwork is your ability to get along with others to achieve common goals. If you think you lack the skills to be a team player, act. You can get the benefit from your team to sell more as well as advance your career!

Answering the below questions will help you understand the critical aspects of your job. This will increase your focus on getting better at what you have been hired to do and stop wasting your energy on things you should not be doing in the first place!

<u>QUESTIONS FOR LEARNING</u>

1. What are the key products and services I can offer to my customers?
2. What are the key features of my offering that differentiates it from the competition?
3. Which customers am I visiting in the next 30 days? What should I sell them?
4. Will this customer pay? How do I make sure that they will pay?
5. Who are the other people in my company that can contribute to my success?
6. How should I work with them closely?
7. How can I make my boss' life easier?

<u>*NEXT STEP*</u>

Once you have a good understanding of why you have been hired, let's jump into making your business plan in the next chapter.

You should be able to visualize and condense your sales potential for a specific time on a piece of paper.

5

Business Plan

How do you make sure that you strive to fulfill what you have been hired to do every day? How do you set realistic goals and decide what actions to take? Are good intentions enough to keep the competition out?

Most companies fail not because they have a poor product, but because they have poor sales.

Welcome to the business plan! You need one, whether you like it or not!

In simple words, it is a customer, product, and market-specific document that links how much money can be made by the business to the actions needed to make that money.

The ability of a salesperson to make a realistic business plan is a good benchmark of how well they know the customers, market, and the potential of the product or services.

The key to sales success is **revenue growth**.

Make sure you're addressing this in all business plans – how do I grow my business? Your job is to bring the maximum amount of money for the company, or yourself if you are the business owner.

Your business plan should be written in **simple** and easy to understand language. Whether it's you or your CEO reading it, the plan should be easy to understand.

This means it must be **short**! Resist the temptation to write essays and lots of descriptions and explanations. You could use simple charts or diagrams to convey your points.

The plan should be **realistic** and achievable. It should be challenging enough, so you and your team go the extra mile to achieve it.

All the above is a waste of time without concrete **actions** with realistic deadlines.

If you are a sales leader, make it mandatory for your people to limit their business plan to a maximum of 10-15 pages or slides.

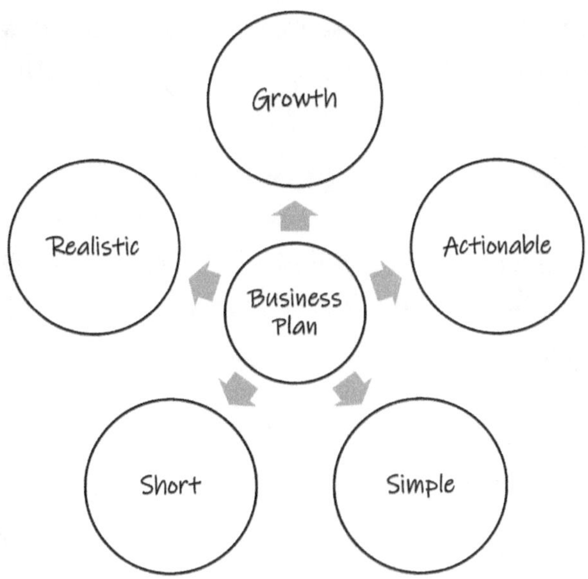

This may be hard to do, but it comes with a benefit. When people need to think hard to keep things short yet include everything they want to communicate in their plan, they start prioritizing.

"Everything" gets replaced by "things that matter most," and this has a significant impact on the success of the business plan itself.

Let's discuss some good questions your business plan should answer. These are applicable for a business plan for-

1. One customer
2. One region with many customers
3. One Technology or product sold worldwide
4. The whole Company

When you read and start filling out the answers, don't forget to be simple, short, realistic, growth, and action-oriented!

Business Plan questions

How much business I had in the last 5 years? What is the potential for the next 3-5 years?

____

____

What growth percentage am I targeting? What assumptions am I making?

____

____

What are the most critical 2-3 current market trends? Where do we stand?

____

____

What is the maturity level of my technology or product?

____

____

What are the other disruptive technologies being developed that could kill my business or technology?

Who are the top 20% of my customers that will make 80% of my sales? What measurable action plans should I make for them?

What experience should I use to get better results? Do the past numbers indicate any trend I could use for the future?

How are my competitors perceived by the customer?

What actions and deadlines will help me achieve my goals? Which internal resources will I need to accomplish my goals?

Below are some considerations

Business History

Why worry about the past 3-5 years' numbers? Numbers never lie, and they are a great way to know where you stand.

They tell you a few important things-

- Your order intake and profits
- Most important customers who make up the majority of your business
- Your best and worst selling products, technologies, and salespeople
- Your market share and how the competition is doing in the same markets

This information is a treasure that you can leverage to boost future sales. Avoid repeating past mistakes and do things differently.

Growth

The crux of a business plan is to achieve growth, i.e., make maximum money. Everything that is included in the plan must point to making more profits.

Buying Philosophy

Every customer has some internal guidelines on how to purchase, including how to evaluate the different suppliers. You will be able to price your product and pitch your value proposition more effectively after you know their buying philosophy.

Stakeholders

Selling is all about people selling to people! It is rare to have one person deciding everything from your customer's side, and hence, your task is to map the stakeholders as soon as you can!

Competitors

Most often, you are not the smartest salesperson, and your company is not the best supplier all the time. Your customers always have options, and they use them from time to time. It would be beneficial to know what actions your competitors are undertaking to keep you from winning in the future.

Actions and Deadlines

All the above is useless without actions with clear deadlines. A sense of urgency must be created.

Market Trends

When you are handling a full region with many clients, find out some key market trends that could help bring more business. Ideally, these trends should help you identify specific problems your clients will be facing in the future.

For example, let's say that the local government wants to implement some regulations to reduce pollution. This means your customers will have to make changes in the way they operate their factories. This is an opportunity for you because they will have to allocate their time and resources to solve this problem and will have to act.

Another example could be sustainable energy. Maybe your customers need to meet their electricity needs by producing at least 20% solar power. This is again a customer problem that could boost your business if you are in the solar business.

Customers are always catching trends that make them more profitable or help them meet regulations set by the local government. Your task is to exploit them fully.

Maturity Levels of a product or technology

For any technology or product, four stages dictate the pricing and resource allocations.

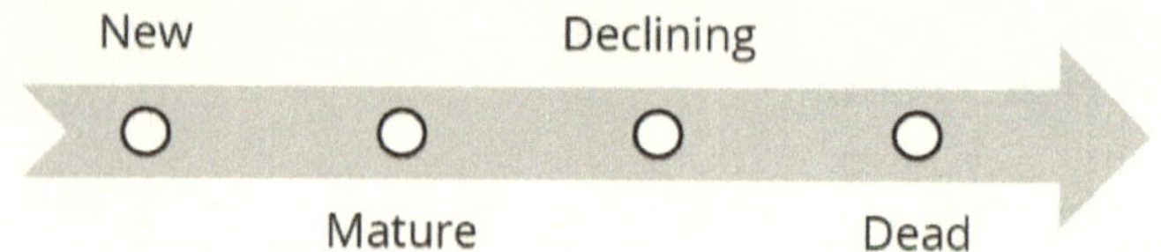

1. New Technology / Product

If you are launching a new technology, you are like a start-up! You have probably tested this technology at a pilot level and do not have commercial experience. This stage requires you to look for customers who will "try" your technology inside their business. It could also be a new piece of software you just created that needs some customers before you can grow it further. You must put your best resources on this technology or product. You could also try to find some collaborative partners who could assist you in making this technology widely accessible worldwide. All these actions must be included in your business plan.

2. Mature Technology / Product

If you have a commercially proven technology with many references, then it is stable and mature. Your business plan should address how you improve your market share as well as how you could develop this further.

Your market intelligence should also be able to find what disruptive technologies are being developed. If your competitor brings such technology to the market, it can kill you in no time!

3. Declining Technology / Product

No matter how cool a technology appears in the beginning, the competition catches up, and before you know it, there are many players in the market that offer similar features as you but at lower prices. This is the time when you must decide on how much profit you can realistically get from this product and how long you wish to continue with it! If you have a better product already developed, when do you launch it? Have you included all this in your business plan?

4. Dead Technology / Product

You will know if you are selling a dead technology or product if some of the below scenarios happen to you frequently-

- Your sales, and hence profits, are dropping every quarter. Your salespeople give you this feedback from time to time!
- The majority of your sales are by offering huge discounts
- There is hardly any technical discussion with your customers! It's always the price!
- Your team cannot even find three features of your product that differentiate it from your competitor
- Your customers don't send their high- level people to your meetings

Many companies struggle to see this objectively. Since they have invested capital and resources in developing and selling this product, it is hard for them to pull the plug. As a salesperson, you have a responsibility to give the correct feedback on the matter.

Even if you're in a declining industry, or your products are not competitive, remember that you are always going to be asked to sell them and more of them.

Your business plan must reflect the current stage of your technology or product.

The business plan is a great tool to understand your current position in the market, set new goals and critical actions to make more money in the future.

> ### QUESTIONS FOR LEARNING
>
> 1. How do I make an effective business plan?
> 2. Which assumptions in the business plan have to be proven correct to achieve success?
> 3. How do I set up targets and actions to achieve my business plan objectives?
> 4. How do I measure the outcomes of targets and actions?
> 5. What feedback mechanism is built into the business plan? How frequently should I revisit the plan?
> 5. Am I missing something obvious?

<u>*NEXT STEP*</u>

Good intentions don't bring business. Without goals and actions, your business plan will remain on paper. The next two chapters will show you how to do them effectively.

6

Where to Shoot?

After the business plan is ready, it is time to set goals or targets for yourself. Whether you are handling one customer or a region with many customers, achieving your targets will help you grow your business in line with the company business plan.

How to set up goals and targets?

Employment needs to be a win-win situation. This means your employer grows their business because of your contribution, and you, in turn, gain experience and a sense of accomplishment and learning. This also holds true if you are a business owner. This implies that the goals and targets are set up to reflect this win-win philosophy. This is one of the keys to having an engaging job that provides a lot of motivation for you to challenge yourself and raise the bar. For the employer, this is the way to create loyalty and improve job satisfaction.

Below are some of the factors to be considered while setting up goals and targets-

1. Matching capabilities and goals-

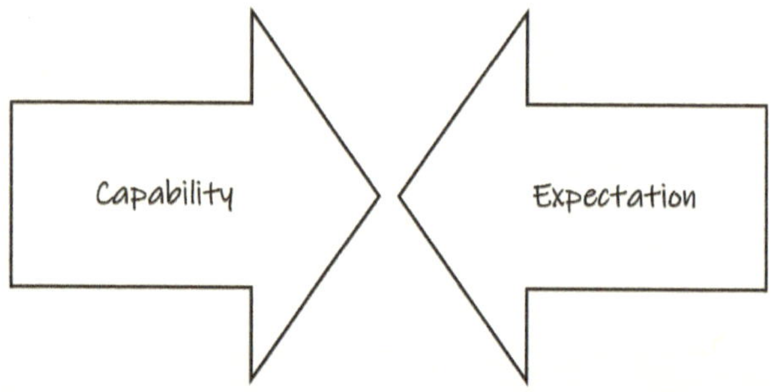

The ability of your manager, as well as yours, to match your capability with the goals and targets set for you is one of the most fundamental factors that will determine whether you could achieve these targets.

This will also help you identify your improvement areas and give your employer the opportunity to train you in those areas.

If you are being delegated tasks and responsibilities without a clear assessment of your strengths and weaknesses, you must seek the support of your manager. This will help you in the long run and foster teamwork.

Talking about capability, there are two approaches to

accomplish most business tasks-

1. Do your best and complete the task.
2. Find out the best version of the completed task and then make efforts to complete it.

The second approach requires you to think about the quality of the finished task and stretch yourself to achieve it. This approach will also help you raise your capabilities and competencies continually.

For example, assume you have to make a presentation to a prospect for a million-dollar deal. The best possible outcome of this presentation is that you convince the customer and close the deal. Now, start working backward on your presentation. Make sure that every slide takes you toward closing the deal. The benefits you offer, including the numbers, should stand out. This way, you will stay focused, and your presentation will impress the prospect.

2. Challenging yet Realistic expectations including numbers-

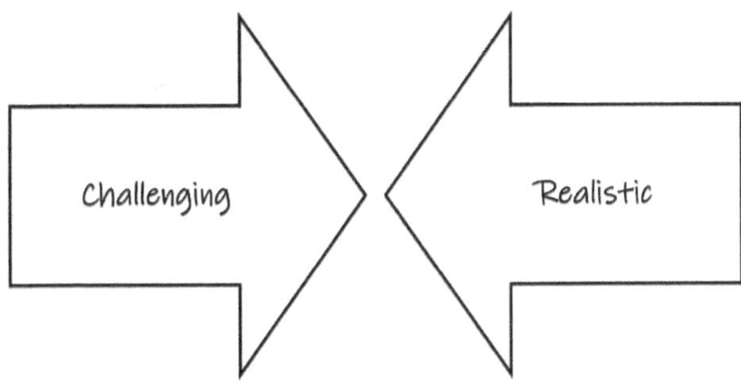

Sales is a numbers game, and you must get better at playing it to win. Your yearly targets should include a certain amount of business that you must bring in. This is also motivating as it sets a clear direction for you to engage in productive actions that bring you the numbers.

To show your accountability. Try to engage in discussions with your manager and have a say in how much business you are expected to bring.

Since nobody can predict the future (including consultants and data scientists), you and your company have to make some assumptions that are part of this goal setting. It is crucial to have them clearly understood both ways.

The numbers you need to achieve should be challenging enough, requiring you to stretch yourself and try innovative ideas to win business. At the same time, they must be realistic and doable. If not, your job becomes impossible and will drain you of energy. You won't last long in that job!

Ideally, you should have the right mix of three types of customers-

1. Loyal Customers
2. Customers on the fence
3. Potential customers who typically don't buy from you!

If you have only loyal customers as your prime responsibility, who bring you a continuous business without bringing in any competition in the buying process, you will become complacent. That does not mean there is no growth potential from loyal customers. It is just that you also need some difficult customers to grow your sales skills.

For example, if you are meeting targets every year with little traveling, it means you have comfortable clients! So, if you are handling very easy and only loyal clients, talk to your manager and ask for some difficult ones like the ones who are on the fence every time they need to purchase something as well as those who never buy from you. While this seems counterintuitive, remember your goal- you want to become a highly effective salesperson and bring maximum money to your company. This means you need to stretch yourself and put yourself into situations that are always not in your comfort zone.

For customers on the fence, meet them often, and understand their problems. Tell them that you have cost-effective solutions, and you can discuss them in more detail. During the discussions, give them confidence by showing references and other good work you have done on similar problems.

On the other hand, if you have mainly clients who never buy from you, and you are expected to "suddenly" start getting business from them, your job could become impossible.

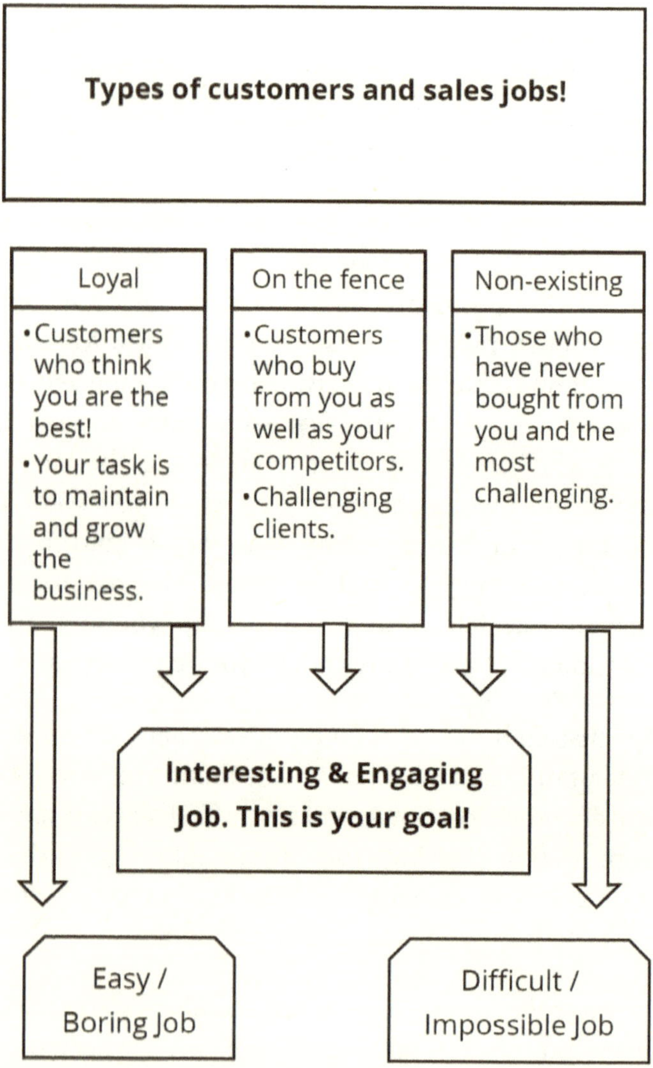

If you can win business from some of them, it will bring growth in your market share and revenue because this customer never bought from you before.

For these "non-existing" clients, make some cold calls, and find out how your competition is serving them. If you find any loopholes, whether it's bad service, overpriced products, or late response, begin there. Start talking about other customers where you have replaced the competitor's product with yours and what benefits your clients are getting. Offer to arrange a phone call between the two and let the magic of reference sales work its way. This is not as difficult as it seems.

There is a fine line between the challenging clients who are open to switching over to you as opposed to those who simply keep buying from your competition and intend to do so in the future.

With a few visits, you will understand which side you are dealing with!

It is crucial that you get this customer mix right, and talk to your manager if you think it is not optimal. Feeling motivated at your job is your prime responsibility, and you must act if you are short on motivation.

3. Adjustment and feedback mechanism-

Most companies have employee appraisal procedures once or twice a year. Depending on your situation, this could be a breeze or a horror!

Example- Suppose you had a below-expected performance in a year. If you and your manager realize that some critical aspects of work were missing at the end of the year, then you were probably not talking to each other often enough.

There must be ample room for feedback and adjusting the course of your actions to meet the goals and targets that have been set for you. This could be in the form of 1:1 meetings every 15 days or once a month between you and your manager and other stakeholders in your company. This way, you will also feel inclusive in the process of achieving the goals. Simultaneously, your manager will also have enough time to guide you to achieve your goals. Of course, this should not become like an appraisal where you prepare for a week and spend a lot of time that should be utilized in meeting clients!

1:1 meetings are also the right forum to measure the outcomes of your goals and actions.

If you have even the slightest leadership aspirations, you must learn to give and seek active feedback.

On the other hand, if there are no feedback mechanisms in your company or your team, you could bring this to the attention of your management. If no action is taken, you must question whether you are working for the right leader or the right company.

4. Teamwork-

Nobody sells alone! While you might think you are

facing the clients, and hence, what you do decides which way the business goes, it is not entirely true! To succeed, you will have to seek help and support from your colleagues. A good manager will make sure your targets will require you to rely on the expertise of a few other people in your organization.

Fostering teamwork to get the best out of each team member's strengths is the key to get staggering sales. Teamwork will also help cover your weaknesses as a salesperson and help everyone in the team feel inclusive in achieving the common goal.

Example- If you are doing project selling, you will have different departments in your company helping you realize the sale. If you think you can do it all by yourself, you haven't understood your role yet!

5. Self-development-

It is usual for a company to expect a lot of things from you that will help them grow business. But what about you? You also have your career and learning ideas and goals to help you become better at selling.

Be sure to include some self-development goals in your annual targets. Take stock of what you want to become in the long run and align your targets accordingly.

If you need the training to learn new things or polish specific skills, mention it in your goals. Your boss cannot read your mind, so you must spell it out clearly.

Put aside an hour every week for personal development, no matter what.

Many salespeople mistakenly believe that it is the responsibility of their company and manager to look after their career and development.

Your career growth is your responsibility.

QUESTIONS FOR LEARNING

1. Do I have a realistic target and a reasonably good customer base? If not, how do I address these points?
2. Which of my skills need improvement that will help me achieve the targets?
3. How do I use the feedback mechanism to perform better at my job?
4. Am I a team player? If yes, how do I foster more teamwork and use it to win more business? If no, what should I do to improve?

NEXT STEP

The only way you can achieve your goals is by taking the right actions. We will learn what those actions are and how to complete them in the next chapter.

7

Hustle!

Your business plan addressed essential factors that will help you grow business. After you have set up realistic yet challenging goals and targets, let's devise an action plan to achieve them.

Actions speak louder than words. They always do!

Just do it!

Make a deliberate habit of being biased toward taking actions than making plans or strategies. The benefit of this approach is that you can fail fast and learn fast.

Taking actions will also reduce your stress and motivate you toward achieving your goals. Actions are the antidote to negative thinking, and you can experience this only by making a start. Just act!

For example, let's say you are unsure whether to visit

a prospect who does not buy from you. Rather than thinking over the pros and cons and which strategy you should have, just show up!

Once you have a conversation going on, you will figure things out. And who knows, this prospect may be fed up with your competitor and looking to switch over!

In general, most of your time and energy should be spent on trying to achieve the desired goals and as little as possible on other activities.

This is easier said than done, and therefore, you should consider basing your actions on the below important criteria.

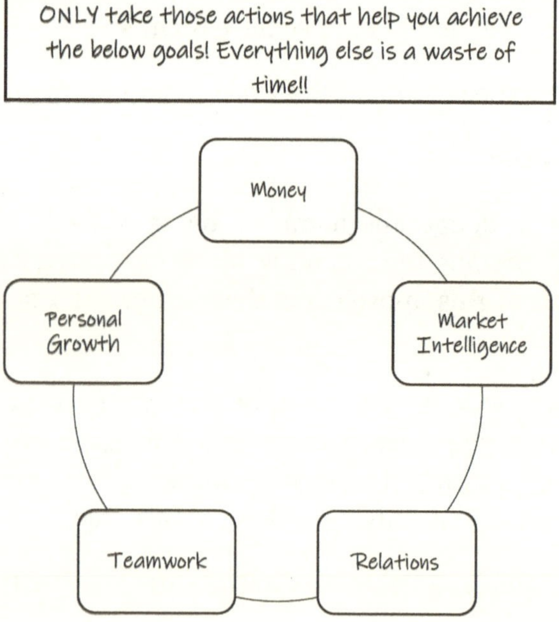

1. Actions that bring money!

Since you have clear goals, every action you take every day must improve your chances of making maximum money for your company. This, obviously, means that anything you do that does not take you toward this target must be thought through, and the decision made whether to continue doing it.

Focus on below actions-

- Meeting clients
- Understanding client problems and providing them with solutions
- Prioritization of clients
- Close follow-up till you win or lose the sale

If you are unsure about which customers to visit, begin by spending at least 40% of your time outside your office and computer screen i.e., with your customers. Over time, you will know them better, and you will know how to prioritize them.

Alternatively, below are four categories of customer visits that will improve your chances of winning more sales.

A. Visiting customers with immediate problems to solve

When you know of such customers, visit them as a priority to understand their problems. It may be likely that they have the budget and resources allocated to solve this problem. This means you can close the sale quickly, provided you have a compelling value proposition.

B. Visiting your existing customers

If your existing customers have a problem with your service or goods you have just supplied, don't avoid them. It is vital that you visit them and solve the problem. This way, they will know that you are a responsible salesperson and will also support them in the future.

Even if things are great, you must visit your customers regularly. Your competitors are knocking on their doors from time to time!

Sometimes, such visits will help you start a new conversation about a problem you have solved for your other customers. It might lead to more business from this customer.

C. New prospects

No matter how effective and enthusiastic you are about your sales job, there will be people who don't buy from you!

To increase your market share and grow faster than the market is growing, these customers are your best shot! Visit them to find out what they do, how they buy, and how you can help. You might succeed this time!

D. Networking events

Whichever business you are in, there will be some conferences and exhibitions where your customers, subject matter experts, and your competitors gather to discuss industry trends and other important aspects.

Show up in these networking events and actively participate by presenting something or have a booth that will attract the right customers. Once you get some new contacts, follow-up and visit them. These events will also help you grow your network and help you learn more about your business and the market.

Make sure that you understand these four categories of customers and distribute your time wisely to win more business.

2. Actions that help you Gather Market Intelligence

Since you and your company operate in a market where your competitors are also trying to win their share of the business, you must have up to date market information. Once you have that, you must devise a plan to make good use of it.

Many salespeople make their sales strategies without

doing a proposer market analysis. This leads to a bias toward actions that are in their comfort zones and can leave out some crucial actions that can really make the difference.

The below actions can help you get the market intelligence-

- Understanding market trends by talking to clients regularly
- Learning about new regulations and their impact on the market and your business
- What is the competition doing?
- Subscribe to websites that provide data

3. Actions that help build client relationships

Your customers always don't make rational decisions.

People buy from people they know and trust. Building trust is not something that happens overnight and requires some planning and conscious effort.

In a later part of this book, we will talk about selling based on a strong value proposition. But to convince the client about the value of your solution, you need more than just numbers and a great story. Your good relationship with the client will be of excellent service here.

Focus on below actions-

- Coaching your clients to make better buying decisions
- Collaboration with clients- You can work with your client to develop a new technology or product or service concept
- Seeking feedback on your products and services
- Arranging a high-level management meeting between your company and the client
- Socializing with the clients

4. Actions that help grow teamwork

It is useful to factor in teamwork during the goal setting.

If you start helping others regularly, you will make plenty of friends and will be labeled as "team player."

Focus on below actions-

- Actively engage your team members in problem-solving
- Seek and give feedback from time to time
- When you get a sale, give them due credit for their work!
- Attend every family event if your company has them!
- Don't be a lone wolf!

- Don't play politics! Your team members will find out sooner or later!

5. Actions that help you grow yourself

Since you have set the bar high for your learning and growth, your actions should reflect the same.

Leaving one's comfort zone or making a new comfort zone at a higher level than you are today will act as a catalyst for growth and satisfaction in your career.

This will require you to do an honest self-assessment from time to time and seek support from other people, including your boss.

Focus on below actions-

- Learn new skills and acquire new knowledge
- Be known in the market
- Seek feedback about how you are doing, even if you are meeting the numbers

As you implement these actions, your results will start improving. Very soon, you will be winning lots of business, even from the clients who never bought from you before.

Despite all this, if you are short on motivation, just start calling and visiting as many clients as you can. Do it for a month, and slowly, you will start to build momentum. If you do it for six months, you will have enough things to keep yourself busy. You will start getting calls from these customers to solve their problems. They will be eager to meet you. You will start selling more.

QUESTIONS FOR LEARNING

1. Which 2-3 necessary actions should I take this week that will improve my business?
2. What support from my other colleagues do I need to execute these actions effectively?
3. This month, which clients should I visit?
4. Which projects has my competitor won recently? Why did I lose?
5. Which learning areas I should focus on this year?
6. Which 20% of my actions will produce 80% of my results?

NEXT STEP

Your goals and actions have a better chance of succeeding if you are good at time management. The next chapter will show you different types of "times" and how to balance them. Keep reading.

8

Are You On Autopilot?

A business plan is just the beginning of your journey for the entire year. You also have set up the goals and actions that will complement the business plan. But have you thought about your time allocation to different activities you are required to do as a salesperson? Before you can even think of optimizing your time, take stock of where and how you spend it.

Only after that will you be able to decide which activities should be stopped and which ones be prioritized. This will bring a sense of continuity to your productivity at work and will show up in your daily work and yearly results. This will save you from being on autopilot at work! Stopping unproductive activities requires the right level of self-awareness, humility, and a willingness to make bold decisions. Since you want to sell more and be productive at work, this must be done.

When it comes to your job as a salesperson, your time is generally the sum of the below –

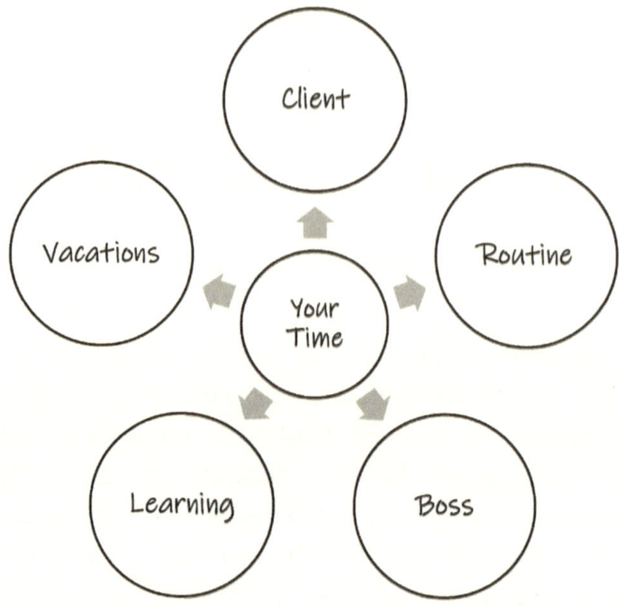

Let's understand what each category of time means!

Client Time

For you to bring more business, your client time should only consist of the following activities-

- Client meetings
- Preparing a value proposition for the client
- Talking to your clients and writing relevant emails

- Making effective action plans to make more sales

You must be able to inform your customers of something useful when you meet them. It could be anything that makes their life more comfortable, such as solutions to their problems, potential problems they could face and how to solve them, or some new market trend. Also, when you visit the client as a team, make sure that you have an active role in that meeting, and you are not just sitting while your colleagues do the talking.

Preparing for meetings is also equally important. For example, suppose you are making some slides for a client meeting. Ask yourself what message you wish to convey and how the finished slides should look. Avoid distractions such as emails or talking to your colleagues. Learn to say no to any other activity or person that can take your focus away from what you are doing.

When you guard your time and focus on completing one task at a time, your results will improve. Others will know your style of working, and hence, won't distract you when you are busy. They might start consulting you on how you can get so much done at the same time.

Try this for one week. Start questioning yourself on each activity you do. You will be amazed to learn the different aspects of how you spend your client's time.

This will also give you an opportunity to evaluate things you are doing right, things you need to improve, and things you should stop doing completely!

Not everything can be urgent, although most clients make it look so. With experience, you will also know which client requirements are urgent and which are not.

Routine Time

You must take a hard look at what routine means to you and how to make it more effective, so you produce great results.

While this is a broad category, and the place where most of the time and energy could be wasted, you must learn to be efficient here.

Your routine time should only consist of the below activities-

- Internal Meetings with a clear agenda where you add value
- Checking emails in time slots and not continuously
- Making visit reports and expense statements
- Other things you think are essential to generate more sales!

Talking about emails, set a fixed time every day to

check email. Don't check and try to reply to them as and when they land in your mailbox. You might wonder if you will miss urgent emails. Well, No!

If something is urgent for your customers, they will call you. The same goes for your boss or your colleagues, who will ask you directly without waiting for you to read the email. This way, you won't miss anything.

Your focus on doing productive tasks will drastically improve.

Apart from continuously checking emails, internal meetings are the real-time killers. If you work for an organization where it is fashionable to have meetings, you must question and challenge this culture.

Below are the only internal meetings you need to attend-

- Meeting with a clear agenda where have some role
- Feedback sessions such as sharing valuable experiences
- Meetings that help grow business or solve problems
- Meetings that foster team building

When someone asks you for a meeting or sends an invitation, talk to them before you accept. Without being rude, ask what your role is and who are the other people attending the meeting. Do it a few times! This one habit will make your colleagues understand that you value your time, and they will only invite you for important meetings.

As time goes by, your results will start speaking for themselves, your influence within your team will start growing, and others might start reducing the number of meetings!

Beware of this timewaster that is meetings without a clear agenda and guard your time! You could be a little creative and put some Dilbert cartoons about meetings in your office. Others will get your message!

There must be many other activities you are doing as routine. Take time to write them down and decide whether these activities help you generate more sales. If not, discard them. You will be surprised to learn that your routine time will start shrinking, giving you much more time for other activities.

Boss Time

This is an interesting topic! Your manager plays a considerable role in your career growth as well as in the development of you as a salesperson. Also, most of the boss's time is boss imposed, and you might not have much room to maneuver.

The good part is that your manager also has targets to meet, and you are an important asset to help them achieve those targets. You must use this to optimize your time spent with your manager.

Cultivate a habit of thinking one or two levels above where you are. Put yourself in your boss' shoes and see things from his perspective. This "helicopter view" will help you understand what is important to your boss and how you could help.

Predominantly, your boss time should be used for-

- Keeping them informed on what you are doing
- Seeking their feedback and support
- Discussing your plans and actions to grow business
- Building a rapport with them
- Discussing conflicts, if any.

Since your goal is to become a damn good salesperson, you should aim to work for bosses who are great at selling or have exceptional leadership skills, or preferably, both.

Self-development time

What? You might ask!

For you to stand out among the crowd in the longer run, you must continually develop yourself. Markets

are always changing, and what worked yesterday won't necessarily work tomorrow. Hence, today is the time to take stock of the situation and learn new things that are necessary for your survival and success.

Try to spend time on the following-

- Learn more about your product, market, and business
- Learn skills that will complement your job, such as attending courses or watching videos on communication and presentation skills, body language, or any other skills
- Ask yourself hard questions about what you should stop doing from time to time
- Networking among colleagues

Don't feel guilty about spending office time on self-development. All your organization wants is excellent results, and that's what you are trying to achieve by taking time for your own development.

Vacations

We live only once! That is a good excuse to take vacations, isn't it? During most of the year, you put your company first and try to get impressive results. But there must be a time for you when you travel and spend time with your family and loved ones.

If you are saving your vacations, so you get cash

rewards when you leave the job or retire, think again! If you are having a great career in sales, you will probably make good money during your working life. What's the use of it if you don't take time off to enjoy your wealth and family? You might be getting too old to enjoy vacations.

If it is difficult for you to take up this conversation with your boss, think about the benefits you get out of vacations and the value you provide to your company with your great work.

ACTIONS FOR LEARNING

1. What is my time distribution among the five categories discussed in this chapter?
2. Which unproductive time can be saved and converted into productive time? How?
3. Which activities should I stop doing altogether?

NEXT STEP

Excelling in what we have learned so far will help you build a strong foundation and improve your career and the chances of more sales. Next, we will talk about customers and how to sell effectively.

PART III:

SHOWTIME

Start selling more!

9

Crush It!

Let's say that you are trying to sell software that could help your client cut their costs by 20%. You have priced the software competitively and believe that the client will understand this, and you believe you will win the sale.

When you meet the client, you start talking about how great your company is and how excellent its products and services are. You do the most talking as if the client is clear on what you are offering. A few days later, you learn that you are not getting this order! What went wrong?

It's time to talk about the elephant in the room- **Value Proposition!**

Your business plan, targets, and goals have no chance of succeeding if you don't make a habit of understanding the value proposition you bring to the customer.

Let's understand this in more depth to fully make use of it and win a lot more business!

Saleable Value Proposition!

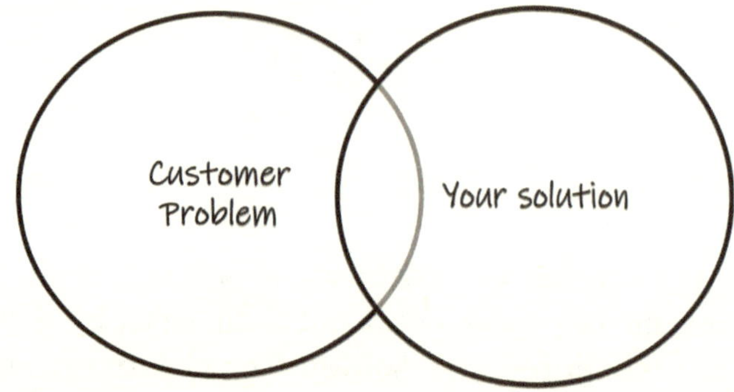

You haven't understood the problem...yet!

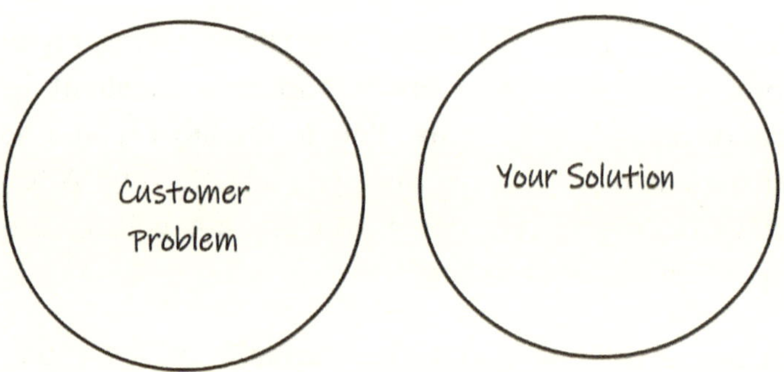

Are you the right salesperson?

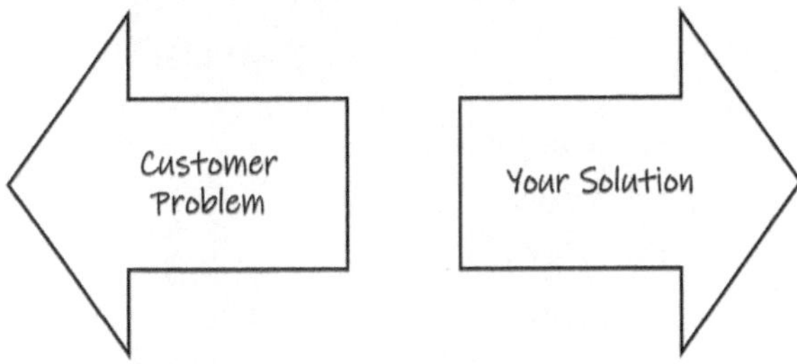

What is Value?

It can be defined in 2 ways-

1. What you offer that will be useful to someone
2. What you offer that will be useful to the client for which the client will pay you money or exchange something because it's worth it!

In the first case, your value proposition does not necessarily convert into a business. Example- If you want to do some charitable activity or run a non-profit, you offer value to someone by helping them but expect no money in return. But you still must figure out what the value is and how you can offer it.

The second case is purely a business case, where you are looking to get money in exchange for your or your company's product or service. It is tough to get anyone to pay for your ideas if they are not useful to them.

After you fully understand the true meaning of value,

it's time to learn how to find value and how to formulate your value proposition. Below are the five ingredients to make a great value proposition-

1. Identify the problem
2. Importance vs. Urgency
3. Customer's options
4. Your solution
5. Your differentiation

1. What are the problems or pain areas of my client?

A potential client is willing to spend time, resources, and money on one or more of below three things-

A. To increase their profits

Example- They want to implement new software that will cut costs, and thus, contribute to more profits.

B. To fix the problems that cost something valuable such as safety or job security

Example- Companies that are running into losses and wanting to fix their business processes.

C. To meet some regulations

Example- An oil refinery wanting to reduce emissions to meet the environmental ministry guidelines. This won't necessarily result in more profits, but it is essential to keep their business running. It could also be to make a green image for their business.

In all cases, the client or individuals have some pain areas that you, as a smart salesperson, must find out. Without it, you have very slim chances of selling anything!

2. How important is the pain area? How urgent is it?

Urgency and importance are two different things.

Problem-1: Very important and needs to be solved but not very urgent.

Problem-2: Less critical than Problem-1 but much more urgent.

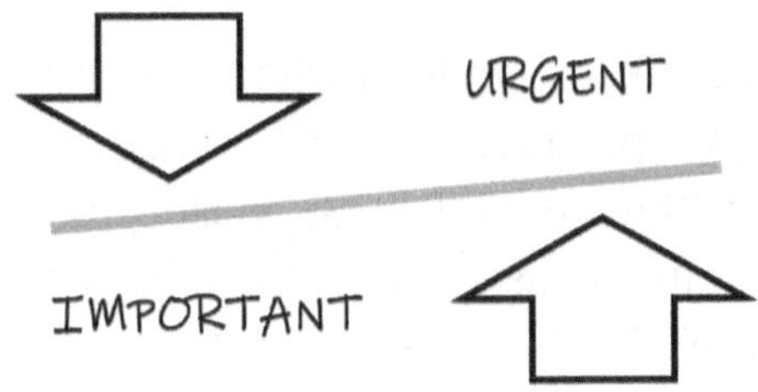

vs

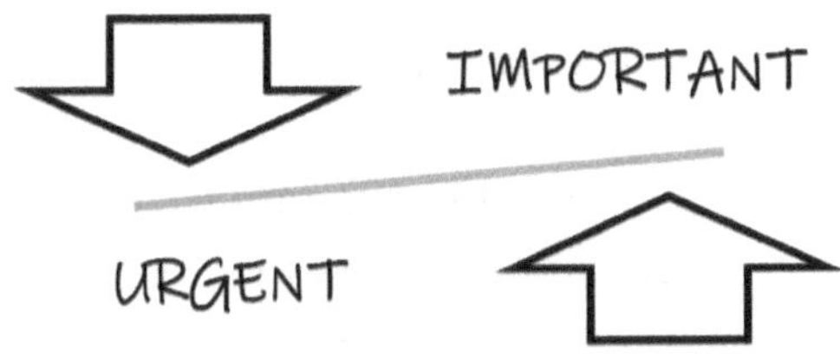

Depending on your client, they will prefer one over the other in terms of allotting their resources and money. Before you even think of pursuing the problem and finding a solution, you must assess the urgency and importance of the pain area of your prospect. This will help you put your energy into prospects that will materialize faster and will keep you away from time wasters. There are plenty of them!

For example, your customer runs a power plant. The customer knows that one of the pieces of equipment in the plant is nearing the end of its life. This can cause production losses if not replaced in time. The cost due to production loss could be multiple times the cost of the equipment. This problem is both urgent and important and is likely to secure a budget.

A more difficult example is when you are proposing an expensive product that will give only marginal benefits to the customer. Suppose your customer uses a piece of software that does the job. You have better software that you think will make the customer's life easier than today. When you start pursuing this opportunity, the customer understands the importance of the upgrade. But since their current software is doing the job, this problem is not urgent. Your task as a salesperson is to find problems or potential problems this customer could face with the existing software and create an "urgency" for them to buy your software.

3. What are your client's options? Do they have a budget allocated?

A client has a problem to be solved, and it is quite important and urgent. Now, they are talking to you as well as your competitors to develop a solution. This is the time to think about what options are available to the client.

There must be a budget allocated if the problem is important and urgent. Without it, either the client is not serious, or they might have an option for not doing anything for the time being. They will engage you and your competitors, figure out a few solutions, and make a nice report to submit to their bosses where it will gather dust for a long time!

Your time is precious, and you have targets to meet. You must avoid getting into flow with the client without being sure that there is a clear budget and a mandate to fix the problem. If you are not, ask them questions. Make them aware by your actions that you want to help but also want their money for your time.

If you are unsure, you could use delaying tactics without losing the client altogether! Say that your team is busy with other projects, and it will take you more time to submit the quotation. See how they react.

Sometimes, customers want you to include multiple options in your quotation. This can be time-consuming, and some options might not be feasible. Tell them that you need two months to submit your quotation. Keep in constant touch with them and kill options that are not feasible without spending too much time.

4. What solution can you offer?

Now you are convinced that your client has the desire and the means to solve the problem, it's time to go full throttle!

You must formulate your solution in a clear, precise, and easy to understand value proposition. While you want to show the client how great your solution is, the key here is to have a laser-sharp focus on the value that you bring. Everything else is unnecessary!

Example- If the client is looking for a new technology that will help them optimize their business processes, your solution must be focused on the monetary benefits and the robustness of this solution.

You should not try to impress your client too hard. Since they have shown interest in you, it means they trust your company and you especially. Hence, do not try to prove yourself too hard!

5. How do you differentiate from the competition? What are the pitfalls of not doing it effectively?

Most probably, you are not the only person your client is talking to fix their problem. Just like your company, there are other companies equally capable of fixing the problem. And just like you, your competitors also have competent salespeople who are as eager as you to get this sale.

The key here is not just differentiation but a better differentiation than your competitors. Assume that two of your competitors offer a similar solution and at a lower price. What do you do?

Reducing the price is not wise, assuming you have a good value proposition. You must come up with a strategy to make the client understand your value proposition better than your competition's and why it's worth more money! If you have been focusing on value from the beginning and have done your homework well, you will find it.

If you can't find a single differentiating factor, try to remodel your value proposition. Do question yourself and the experts in your organization on how to get some unique perspective on the problem, and then figure out how to present it to the client.

The key here is not to just offer a lower price to close the deal. That's the easy part! The problem with price discounting is that it's a one-way affair! The prices only go down once the value proposition is not strong and convincing enough. The buyer also gets used to getting discounts, and that erodes your value as an effective salesperson.

Example- If you work in businesses where most companies offer similar products, the strategy is to quote a high price and then start discounting it. The idea is to stop where your buyer is no longer pushing further, thinking this is the bottom! The problem here is what value, as a salesperson, are you offering here? What is your image in front of your client when you start lowering the price at the drop of a hat? How credible are you? Is this strategy sustainable?

As a salesperson, it is not a very rewarding experience, and in the longer run, the viability of your company and its products is questionable.

Your strategy is to put yourself in pole position with your unique value proposition that is better than everyone else's. This puts you in a privileged position to command premium pricing.

Once you have figured out a clear strategy, it's showtime!

Presenting your value proposition

After you have spent a reasonable amount of time identifying client pain areas and formulating your value proposition, how do you present this to your client effectively?

There are four different ways-

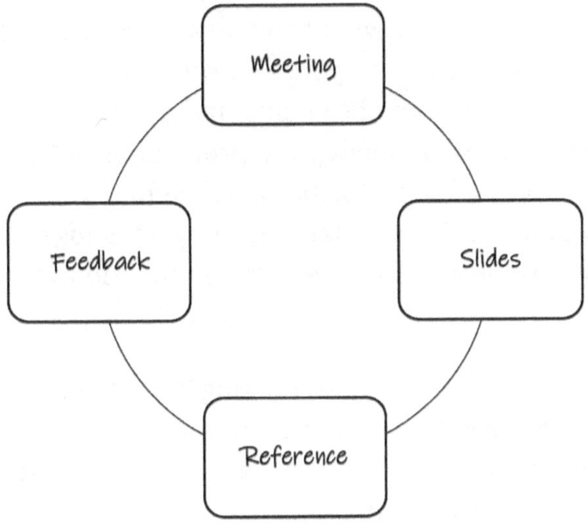

1. Face to face meetings

Show up every single time if the client asks for a meeting!

There is no better substitute for face to face meetings. People like to do business with the people they trust. And a face to face meeting is the ideal way to create and build trust as well as a long-term business relationship. This is true even if the value of the sale is small, and you might think it's not worth the travel cost. You are missing out on an opportunity to build a long-term relationship. The client that has a small requirement today could have a much bigger requirement tomorrow.

Emails and phone calls are an excellent way to start building momentum for your case, but they are not particularly useful when it comes to convincing the client. In fact, if your client wants you to communicate only via emails and phones, they are not serious about solving the problem or not serious about your solution, or both. Therefore, you should request for a face to face meeting to gauge where things are headed and what you should do to win the sale.

You could also consider inviting the client to your office, followed by lunch or dinner. If this offer is accepted, consider that you are one of the serious contenders to close the sale.

Don't pursue the solution if the client is not willing to meet. You won't make the sale anyway! The worse part could be that your solution gets passed on to your competitor, and they make a low-price offer and win the sale!

2. PowerPoint presentations

PowerPoint presentations are not dead yet and won't be anytime soon! If done well, they can drastically improve your chances of winning.

If done poorly, as most people do them, they can be a

dull experience for your client and can kill your chances as well. Have you heard clients talking about some salesperson – the guy with 50 slides! Yes, it sucks! More on this in the next chapter.

3. **Reference**

So, you are trying to break your head in front of your client with the solution. You are almost there but are unsure if the client is 100% convinced.

Think a little differently. Ask yourself if there is some other client who had a similar problem, and you fixed it. See if your happy client, whose problem you solved, would be willing to have a call with this prospective client to share their experiences. If your existing client permits, invite the prospective client for a visit to get feedback about your solution and quality of service. In other words, ask your existing client to help you to sell to this new client. How cool is that!

Also, consider putting good referrals on your website. They will add a lot of value and confidence in what you are trying to sell.

Don't shy away from this strategy if you are sure that your existing client will give a positive recommendation.

4. Feedback

Once you have discussed your solution, try to get feedback from the client. This will show your interest as well as the ability to listen and seek opinions. If you are making a complex sale that requires lots of design work, you must seek feedback from your client from time to time on your proposed solution.

It's funny, but many times, the clients don't know what they want. Hence, never assume that the solution you have given will solve their problem. When you seek feedback, you provide the right conditions for the client to think more deeply about what they are looking for. During the sales process, if you do this well, your client will start trusting you, and this could give you massive leverage over your competitor.

Giving feedback is equally important as seeking feedback. Let's say your client explains the problem in detail. You think you have another client with a similar challenging problem that you helped solve. It could be worth giving some feedback on potential risks based on your experience. You could do this by asking simple questions that will lead the client toward your point or simply saying you had this experience, and you would like to share it with them.

There is another angle to seeking and giving feedback. This has to do with humility. Sometimes, complacency and arrogance can set in your behavior and could be reflected in your approach to the client. If not checked in time, you or your organization could be perceived as challenging to deal with, and this could cost you a lot of business in the long run. When you are humble enough to seek and give feedback, your clients could view you as their extended team member, and your chances of winning will shoot up!

QUESTIONS FOR LEARNING

1. Which pain areas of the client can I solve? Which ones have a substantial monetary benefit for the client?
2. How important and urgent is the problem that my client wants me to solve? Does he have the budget allocated?
3. What are the viable options available to my customer to solve his pain area?
4. How can I solve this problem better than my competitors?
5. How can I use my references and experience in solving the problem for this client?
6. What is the best way to seek and give feedback to my clients about their pain areas?

<u>*NEXT STEP*</u>

In the next chapter, we will learn what the right balance is between talking to your customers and listening to them. How you make killer presentations that will improve customer engagement and your business?

10

Show Them All...?

It's early morning, and you are pumped up because you will be making a presentation today to pitch your idea to potential investo rs or clients.

You have planned to show 40 slides in 1 hour, and you want to be a Rockstar! You imagine the client will be so impressed that you will get the deal in no time.

Now it's showtime. You meet the audience and fire up your PowerPoint presentation. You are raring to go and want to tell your audience everything. You have it all figured out!

To your surprise and disappointment, the below things happen-

- Your audience is sleepy as if they couldn't care less!

- There is hardly any interaction, and they don't have any questions during or after the presentation!
- They tell you just to email your slides after the presentation, and they will keep them in their records [aka we will shift + delete your email because your slides sucked!!]
- They thank you and say they will come back to you when needed. No actions required for now!

What did you do? Where did you go wrong? Could you do better?

Of course, yes!

Content is king!

In the age of YouTube & social media, your clients know a lot about your company and its products. When you are invited to a meeting, you must figure out the clear agenda.

If the agenda requires that you show some slides, it's crucial that you have identified the pain areas of your client or something that they are looking for from you before you even start preparing your slides. Nobody wants to see generic slides showing lots of details about your company.

All they want to see is how you and your products, technologies, and services will benefit them. Don't even start preparing slides until you get this right!

If the agenda is to present your product portfolio to a new prospect, include 2-3 case stories about your key products that this prospect will likely need.

Before you prepare the slides, give careful thought to what the client wants to hear from you rather than what you want to tell them.

Once you know what solution your client is looking for, then it's time to prepare and present the slides to them and convince them that your solution is better than any of your competitors.

Below are six principles that could help you give a killer presentation and a Rockstar sales pitch-

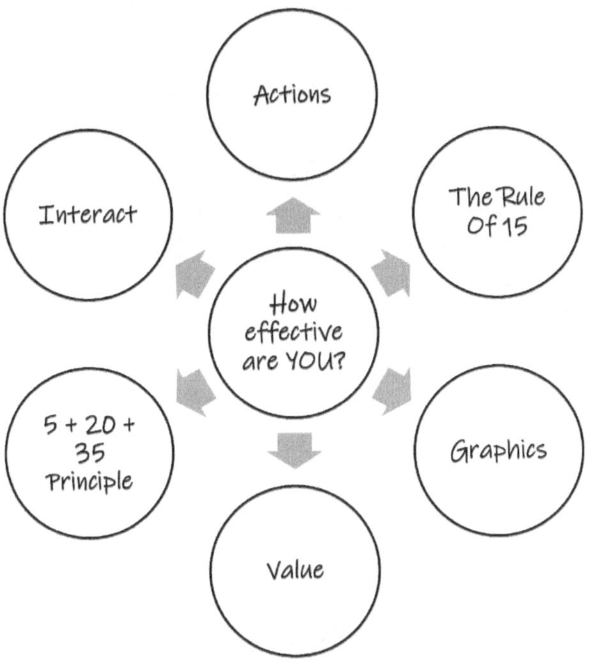

1.   The rule of 15

Your audience has minimal time to grasp your message. Their minds are occupied with their work, boss, family, social events, etc. Some are worried about their next date! This means you have a narrow window to put your ideas into their minds so that they can act upon them. They need to be convinced that the solution or idea that you are pitching will make their life better, and hence, it is worth acting upon.

This means you must be sharp when it comes to showing them your solution.

This is where the rule of 15 comes into play. Keep your slides to a maximum of 15, including the cover and the last thank you slides! You may say you have so much to show, and 15 slides are too few for that, and you will miss out! Well, you must think clearly and purge all the information that you think the client won't need or that will even distract them from the main message.

Out of the 15 slides, try to maximize the number of slides that address solutions to client's problems rather than slides that talk about your company, product, and services. This will make your presentation more specific, which is what your clients are looking for. Everything else is redundant!

Example- Your client is looking for a solution that

will improve the safety and reliability of their factory. You could address this in your slides as follows-

1. Reframe the problem and ask the client whether your understanding is correct
2. How you will solve the problem
3. Timeframe and costs associated with it
4. What benefits the client will get
5. Any other information that could support your claims, such as references

That's it! You don't need to show them any more slides. Your message is unambiguous, and it will cause them to act. You should hear a lot of probing questions and a sudden spark in their interest.

2. Graphics

Writing long sentences on your slides and reading them in front of the audience could put them to sleep! And if you do it while looking at the screen with your back toward the audience, you won't sell anything, and the chances are, you won't get another opportunity to present. Remember that you should be presenting and not reading. They should also not be reading your slides, but rather, trying to focus on you and your message.

Think about it in this way. The goal of each slide is to convey what value you offer to your clients rather than to show them the depth of your knowledge.

When it comes to getting your audience hooked on your presentation, pictures are the key! If everything is written on the slide, then there is no need for you to present in person. You could have just emailed the presentation!

If you have videos, show them to the client. Pause a few times and say a few words, so they get the message.

Pictures speak for themselves and are your key weapons to deliver the message to the audience. Rather than writing sentences on your slides, include some pictures or graphs with 2-3 bullet points incorporating your message. While presenting, explain it at length. If your audience wants further details, prepare a slide in advance to include more information and present it. This way, you will keep yourself on track to present the exact message without getting distracted. (The chances are you won't need this slide.)

3. Value

Since your goal is not just to make this sale but also to sell at good margins, you must understand what value your solution brings to the table and how to make sure that your audience gets it. This will help you when they have liked your solution and want to negotiate on price. If your clients understand that the value your solution provides is way more than the price, it will give you leverage that could help you close the sale with no or minimum discount.

4. 5 + 25+35 Principle

It's a myth that you should do a lot of talking to convince your clients. Your clients don't like to be sold, but rather they like to be led to the solution to their problems. It is your job to understand this and show it in practice during your presentation.

5 + 25 + 35 principle will show you how to do it.

Let's understand this principle and learn how to use it. If you have 60 minutes for the whole meeting, including your presentation, then you should split those 60 minutes as follows-

A. 5 minutes- Introduction and breaking the ice
B. 25 minutes - Maximum amount of time to complete your presentation
C. 35 minutes- Discussion with your client about your solution and further actions

5 + 25 + 35 = Introduction + Presentation + Discussion

You must be wondering if 25 minutes is too short. If you follow the Rule of 15, then you have no more than 15 slides to show. If you are leaning heavily on graphics, then you have enough time to talk about your solution, which means you can easily finish in 25 minutes.

When you devote the last 35 minutes of the time for discussion and answering questions, you send a clear signal to the audience that you are here to listen and solve their problem. They will also open-up and may tell you some other aspects of their problem or a few new pain areas for which they are seeking a solution.

When this happens, tell yourself that your presentation has been a success, and from here on, you are in the driver's seat. From now on, your success or failure to close the sale will depend a lot more on you rather than your clients. The next natural consequence is they start liking you. People buy from people they like and trust.

The next time you visit this client, you could easily see the difference in their approach to your company and your solution.

One side note- It is normal to feel anxious when you start the presentation. Here is a trick to control the anxiety- count from 5 to 1 while breathing deeply. This way, you interrupt your mind's constant thinking that was causing the anxiety.

5. Interaction

If you have followed above four points, then your presentation won't be monotonous. You have made it clear that you have understood your client's pain area and have thought through the solution. You have listened to them actively and want to help them.

Never underestimate the power of listening!

To keep the interest and gauge how they perceive your slides during the presentation, ask them one question per slide and watch their response. When they ask the question, listen, and try to answer it rather than thinking about your next slide.

Sometimes, the discussions will last longer than expected, and you might feel that you will not be able to finish all your slides in the allotted time. That's OK! Just convey the takeaway message from the remaining slides and ask if they wish to know more. This is how you show them that you respect their time but also want to share useful ideas with them.

This will inevitably lead to interactive sessions, and before you know it, your client has already made up their mind to work with you. You have kicked out your competitor by merely being effective in presenting your case.

You could also consider sending your presentation to the client one week before the meeting. This will allow them to prepare in advance and could improve the quality of interactions during the presentation and meeting.

What if you followed the above four points, but the client is not interested? What do you do now?

If this happens, despite your best intentions, you

should ask yourself some questions -

- Is the client serious?
- Have I understood the problem?
- If the solution I am proposing is effective? Is there a better solution?
- Am I meeting the right people? How do I get my solution to the decision-maker?

6. Actions

That brings us to the last rule. Your presentation should generate some concrete actions with deadlines for both you and your client. This is the clear benchmark of whether your client has liked your solution and whether they want to pursue it further.

So, as you approach the end of your presentation, start asking who will do what and summarize the agreed actions just before closing. This will have two benefits-

- It shows your interest in pursuing this opportunity.
- More than this, it shows that the client is serious and wants to devote their time and resources to discuss the matter further. You are one step closer to the sale!

Never leave a single meeting without agreeing on actions.

QUESTIONS FOR LEARNING

1. What is the key message of my presentation? How many slides do I need to deliver this message?
2. How should I stick to the key message and leave everything out?
3. Is the value proposition clear enough for the audience to see?
4. What actions should be agreed at the end of the meeting to take me a few steps closer to the sale?
5. What should I do more of and less of the next time we meet?

NEXT STEP

Learning to make interactive presentations is just the beginning.

The buyer is not the only person you should focus on. In fact, there are many types of stakeholders in every complex sale, and you should develop your senses to understand them better. The next chapter will show you how to do it without freaking them out!

11

❖

Stranger Things!

Let's say you have been working on closing a sale for a while. You have had a few meetings with your client, and you have a good feeling about your chances of winning. The stakeholders are friendly and talk to you regularly. Suddenly, you learn that your competitor won the sale, leaving you clueless. Sounds familiar?

Another example- You have been trying to get meetings with a potential client. You make phone calls, and they say they are busy. They always have some excuse for not meeting you. What should you do?

You think you know all the stakeholders involved in the buying process. You lose a sale and realize that the person you least expected was the primary influencer and that your competitor understood this better than you. Situations like this are not new and can be very frustrating. Can't they?

Welcome to stakeholder mapping! There is always more than what meets the eye in every meeting. As an effective salesperson, it is your task to observe and understand your stakeholders and connect the dots to close the sale. By observing, I don't mean that you be creepy or freak your clients out!

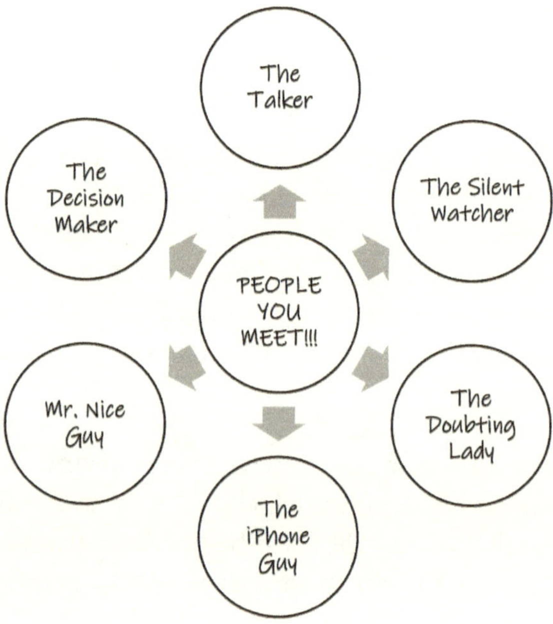

The Talker

This person talks most of the time and is not necessarily the key stakeholder. He may be trying to prove to his boss or colleagues that he knows the subject. You should let them speak, but it's important to let other stakeholders also talk.

The silent watcher

This is the calmest person in the room but could be very influential. Many people talk little or only talk about relevant things. When you encounter such people, you could ask some probing questions to get them talking. They could be an excellent listener and could help you in the longer run.

The Doubting Lady

This person doubts the solution you are proposing and may appear rude. You could be wrong to sideline her. It is rather the opposite. Get into a conversation with her, say you understand her point and stick to your argument if you think you are correct. You will be surprised to know, this is the same person who could help you sell because you listened to her and argued your case professionally. Never fear this person, but rather, try to find one in the meeting.

The iPhone Guy

There will be people who will have absolutely no clue about what is happening in the meeting. They will probably be on their phones or pretending to be listening. You should just focus on other stakeholders without making any comments on this person. You never know when this person gets promoted and sits in a high position! That's life!

Mr. Nice Guy

This is the most helpful person in the room. He is always smiling and sometimes praising your product. Never get fooled by this person into thinking that you are better placed than your competitor to close the sale. Most likely, this person is not a decision-maker, nor has he any influence in the process. He does the same with your competitors.

Decision Maker

While all the above people have different agendas, the decision-maker has a budget and a deadline to meet. While you must try to establish a rapport with them, it is super important (generally) not to bypass key stakeholders, which could be any of the above!

While you are a professional salesperson, who now understands how to map the stakeholders and how to handle them, there will be situations where these people will take you for a ride. They might seek critical information from you and pass it to the competition or simply not give you information that could make your value proposition attractive. If you think this is the case, and you have a compelling value proposition, it's time to reach out to the top guys.

In many organizations, it is the top-down approach,

meaning that it's hard for the middle and lower-level people to say no to what the top bosses are saying.

If you win the sale by approaching from the top, then you must start getting the other stakeholders on your side so that you can repeat the sale in the future. They will understand that you have been smart and will co-operate with you.

People can be irrational, and the decisions they make need not necessarily be logical. But, if you develop a conscious habit of mapping your stakeholders and then play your cards, you could significantly improve your chances of success.

QUESTIONS FOR LEARNING

1. Who are the stakeholders, and what are their roles?
2. Who decides? What are they looking to achieve?
3. What should be the next step to close this sale?
4. How do I sell more after completing this sale?

<u>NEXT STEP</u>

Looking at things from a buyer's point of view will serve you well in your meetings with customers. In the next chapter, we will look into how buyers work and how you could use this understanding to sell more and faster.

12

❧ ⬥ ❧

Buyer's Perspective

While most of the book focuses on selling, let's understand what happens on the other side of the table, i.e., when you are a buyer.

As a buyer, below are some of your responsibilities-

Buying material or services on time

Time is money, and it is your job to plan for things properly so you get the goods and services on time.

Buying at the right price

Money is scarce, and your budgets are limited. But you still need products and services that are reliable. Buying cheap is OK if things you buy serve their intended purpose!

Find money-saving solutions

Money saved is money earned, and you have the possibility to find suppliers who could offer innovative solutions giving you an edge over the competitors of your company!

Commoditizing

This is an interesting one! The pricing strategy of your sellers is based on demand and supply. The fewer your available options are, the higher the price you pay.

As a buyer, you want to reduce the price without

reducing the effectiveness of services and products that you buy.

Commoditizing the products is one of the best strategies you can use to increase the competition and reduce the product and service differentiation. If you do this effectively, the value propositions of your sellers become somewhat similar, which drives down the prices. This way, you get the best of what you need with massive negotiation leverage.

Let's see how to do it! Suppose you have a single supplier for one of your key pieces of equipment. If the equipment breaks down, your production could stop for a few days. Your current supplier knows this, and therefore, is charging you a premium every time you buy the equipment.

Don't fight with them for discounts.

Gather your technical team and invite the top 3-4 competitors of this supplier. Ask them to present their product, references, pricing, and delivery. Approve some of them that fit your expectations and leak this information deliberately to your existing supplier. Very soon, you will see that this supplier wants to talk to you and your management! They are in trouble because they know their competitor also has a great product that could do the job.

Next time, when you have to send an enquiry, invite all approved bidders, including your present supplier. You should see a price drop. This is because by approving 3-4 suppliers on "technical" grounds, you have diminished the leverage of all these suppliers. They are now "equal," and the equipment from any one of them should do a similar job. This is called commoditization, and it drives prices only one way i.e., down.

When your suppliers say that the market is down, they mean that they have little to zero product differentiation compared to the competition!!

Managing your suppliers

You never know when some machine in your plant is going to break down, potentially costing your company millions! This means you try to keep good relations with more than 2-3 suppliers for each of the products and services you need.

You also make sure that compliance is a big agenda when it comes to the ethical behavior of your supplier.

Now that you, as a salesperson, know what buyers want, benefit from this knowledge by making their life easier. Your results will improve dramatically, and you will make lots of connections.

<u>QUESTIONS FOR LEARNING</u>

1. What is the buyer looking for?
2. Which are the constraints and pain areas of the buyer that I could solve?
3. How much should I educate the buyer?
4. How do I develop leverage in this transaction?
5. How do I make the buyer get a win-win deal?

<u>*NEXT STEP*</u>

The most common complaint from the buyer about your company and products is – your prices are very high! In the next chapter, we will learn about pricing and how to answer this question.

13

❬━━━❭

How Much is
Your Worth?

Pricing is an integral part of the value proposition. It is not sufficient to identify the pain areas of the customer and provide solutions. The price you ask should also be reasonable, even if you charge premiums for some products and services.

Your price should not be dictated by how much it costs to produce the product. Your price should be decided by how much comfort you bring to the customer by solving their problem.

In the previous chapter, we learned why and how the buyers commoditize the products and drive the prices down. You have to use this knowledge and prevent or delay this from happening for your products and services. This will give you a premium over your competition.

The challenge is that you don't set the prices yourself as a salesperson. They are most probably set by your management team, and your task is to achieve the price levels and make maximum money for your company.

What is the fair price for your value proposition? How do you find out?

Develop a conscious habit of probing and asking your customers questions to gather useful information. Use this information to build your value proposition.

For example, a prospect calls you for a meeting to discuss possible energy savings for their production plant.

Below are some good "open-ended" questions to ask-

- How do you operate the plant?
- What are your biggest challenges?
- How have you tried to address the energy issue before?
- What are your energy costs?
- What timeline are you seeking to resolve the problem?

Remember not to interrogate the prospect when you ask these questions. Modulate your conversation in such a way that the prospect starts seeing that you are interested and want to understand the problem before proposing a solution.

Now that you have answers to some or most of the questions, you have a solid base to propose one or more solutions. Next, you have to decide the price.

To do that, ask yourself below questions-

- How much money are you helping them save?
- What time will it take for the customer to recover this investment?
- Do your competitors have better capabilities or references where they have solved similar problems based on your experience?
- What is the long-term business potential of this prospect?
- Can you offer 2-3 options at different price points? Each solution should show the prospect how much more money they can make or save.

Repeat the above process for every possible transaction, and very soon, you will develop the habit of winning more business at a premium. Even if your price is the highest, the customer will find it fair as you bring more benefits than the competition.

How to compete with low-cost competitors?

Despite the above strategies, there will be times when a new competitor emerges with ridiculously low prices. This is inevitable.

What do you do?

Your company has three ways to respond to the low-priced product and competitor-

1. Keep a focus on value-based selling without dropping the price levels. In the short term, you might have to sacrifice some market share. The low-price competitor cannot sustain lower prices for long and will have to increase them soon, assuming they are also making quality products that are costly to make. Their management also have profit targets, just like you! Common sense will prevail, and soon, they will also increase the prices to your level.

2. If the competitor comes up with a low cost but inferior product that still gets the work done, then you have a bigger challenge. The competitor is giving the customer the exact quality they need and no more.
    That's when you need to think about your product mix.
    * Do you also launch a similar product?

- Do you continue with the existing product but shift the manufacturing to a low-cost destination?
- How much can cost-cutting help you compete?
- Do you sacrifice profit, accepting that the competitive landscape has changed? Your premium product has diminishing returns for the customers compared to the low-cost competitor product.
- Is it time to kill the premium product, as it is no longer needed?

3. Innovate and look for some disruptive product or service that will put you back in pole position. You will have an opportunity to earn high profits until the competition starts and your niche product becomes commonplace. You need to find new green pastures or a new playing field rather than trying to out-maneuver the low-cost players. This is much harder to do and requires some serious investment, and the ability to take risks on the part of the company. Nothing should be off-limits when it comes to survival!

You might think that this is the task of your leadership team. This is only partly true. You are the eyes and ears of your company and a source of first-hand market intelligence. Also, you have the responsibility to find and show value in your product to the customer. Next time, when you want to give a discount, ask yourself what value are you bringing to the customer?

What if you still can't compete despite trying these strategies?

Quit!

There is no shame in it. It is foolish to cling onto something that has no future. Give yourself a chance for a better future.

Early in your career, decide that you will work for companies that offer premium products and services. This decision could help you to become an expert in value-based selling and have a rewarding career, including monetary benefits.

<u>QUESTIONS FOR LEARNING</u>

1. What is the right price for the problem I am solving for this customer?
2. Have I built a solid value proposition?
3. Does the client understand the tangible benefits of my solution?
4. What general pricing levels the competition is operating?

<u>*NEXT STEP*</u>

Now that you know much more about different pricing aspects, let's talk about price negotiations in the next chapter.

14

—◆—◆—

Give Me More!

Every now and then, you will attend price negotiation meetings or calls. Depending on your leverage, this could be a pleasant or dreadful experience.

There are four pillars of any negotiation-

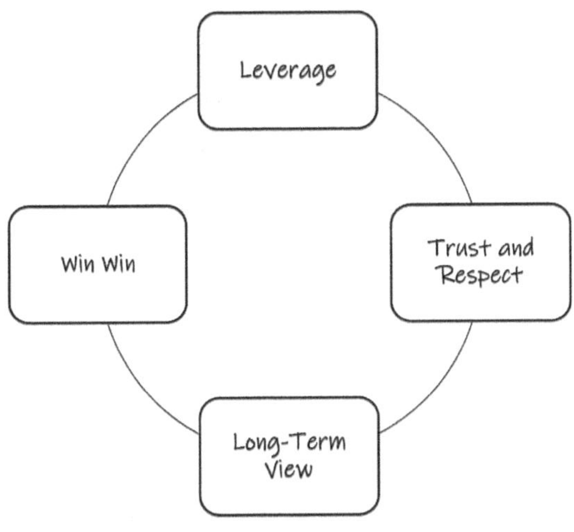

If you are an experienced salesperson, just try to recollect your most significant deals, and you will see that these four factors contributed to them. The reverse is also true for the business you have lost to your competitors.

Let's talk each of the four pillars in detail-

Leverage

Two things can help you gain leverage-

1. Your value proposition, which we have discussed in previous chapters.
2. Urgency for the customer to make decision

Learn to create urgency in the mind of the buyer. Suppose you are in a negotiation meeting where most things except the price have been discussed. Now the buyer says that your price is too high. You were expecting this and give them your well-prepared reply on the value proposition. You try to convince them that they are getting much more than your competitor's proposal- more savings due to your solutions, faster delivery, more guarantees, better services, better reliability, etc. The buyer smiles and says that they will get back to you. What do you do?

Be bold and ask- what will it take to close the deal within one day?

This has two benefits-
A. You show that you need this order.
B. You create urgency for the buyer to say something. It is very hard for them to be quiet when they hear this question.

In most cases, your value proposition will give you leverage, and the deal will be closed quickly at your price expectation.

Expect the buyer to use your price to push your competitors and vice versa. This is part of the game, and you should get used to it. Remember the phone call from the buyer telling you that your competitor is offering a 20% lower price than you. Rather than getting into panic mode, shift the discussion to your value proposition, and soon, the buyer knows you won't take the bait.

Sometimes the buyer comes back saying your competitor has offered a 50% lower price than you. What do you do? If you have done your market and competition analysis well, you will know competitor pricing levels. Also, if the buyer is telling the truth, then why are they even talking to you? 50% is an anchor to put pressure on you and get more than a normal discount from you. The best scenario is again to focus on the value proposition and how you are solving the customer's problem better than your competitors.

Sometimes, you will have to give a little more discount to win a sale. While doing that, you could ask for better payment terms or some other commitment, preferably in writing for the future sale. This way, you will have leverage during the next transaction.

One last thing- If you are not competitive, you should not try to compete! If you cannot find factors that differentiate your service and product from the competition, you must reconsider whether the product is saleable!

Trust and Respect

The fact that you have been called for price negotiation means that the buyer trusts you and your offering. When you start seeing a new prospect, it is important to start building that trust and respect, so when it comes to negotiations, you have a serious shot at winning.

If you see any company with consistently high revenue and income, just understand that they have earned the trust and respect of their customers and are reaping the rewards for doing so successfully.

Because the buyer has a fixed budget and wants to save as much as he can, it is possible that they will bargain very hard and could sometimes be disrespectful. The key here is not to lose your cool.

Tell yourself that these kinds of situations don't last forever.

Long-Term View

Learn to think long term, no matter how stressful the current situation.

Example- If the buyer approaches you for some emergency requirement, this is an excellent opportunity to stand by them. This is also a chance for you to get some extra revenue for the same product. How do you balance it? If you charge a premium, the buyer feels that you are ripping them off. At the same time, if you charge the same price as before, you are not ambitious enough! Take a long-term view and then decide what the right price is and be bold to ask!

Another example is sometimes the buyer will ask for a special discount due to a tight budget. This is a one-off discount only for this transaction and ideally should not apply for the next transaction. The challenge here is when it is time for the next transaction, the same buyer is likely to ask you to continue the discount because you did it once! In situations like these, your leverage, as well as trust and respect for the buyer, will help you take a long-term view and make the decision.

Take one more example from a consulting business. Typically, a consultant is helping to solve the client's pain area by offering some ideas and solutions to implement by their client. Sometimes, the client wants some free consulting and promises that this will lead to more business in the future. The problem is that "free" has no value, and if you agree once, you will have to agree in the future. You must get some commitment from the customer in writing about what business you will get from them in exchange for the free service.

There is one exception to this long-term view if the buying philosophy of the customer has fundamentally changed to purely price-based buying. In this case, decide how much time and energy you want to invest and what are your chances of winning. Don't continue simply because you have already spent a lot of time with this customer. Many salespeople fall into this trap and try to sell things that a customer can no longer afford or need.

Willingness to find a win-win solution

When you start seeing the prospect team and the buyer, try to gauge if they want to find a win-win solution. You might think this is obvious! Why would they not want to do that?

The problem is that the buying process can be complicated, and there are many stakeholders and their agendas. An excellent way to navigate through this topic is to check the buying history of this company.

If they never buy from you, they are most likely fishing for the right solution and pricing from you and then passing it on to your competitors, so they end up winning the business. In such cases, give them a solution without spending too much time on it. Once they have had time to go through it, request meetings, including some high-level management meetings if the sale is big. This approach might nudge the customer to take you seriously if you have a great value proposition

On the other hand, when you see yourself in a commanding position to win an order, it is tempting to demand what you want. You must remember that you want to sell again and again and will come back to the buyer many times in the future. Be reasonable.

Never rip-off your customers!

QUESTIONS FOR LEARNING

1. What does the win-win solution look like in this sale?
2. What arguments should I make to justify the price?
3. How do I close this sale without giving any discount or offering a lower discount?
4. What is my long-term strategy for this customer?

<u>NEXT STEP</u>

By now, you have mastered a simple yet effective technique of finding and presenting value proposition to your customers. You have much more awareness and focus on stakeholder management, presentations, and customer meetings. Over time, this will make you a distinguished salesperson and open leadership opportunities for you. The next section talks about life as a "sales leader."

PART IV:

SLAYING
THE DRAGONS!

Your journey as a sales leader!

15

Legacy

The side effect of becoming an effective salesperson is that you start getting leadership opportunities! When you reach this stage, and someone offers you a sales leadership position, take your time to decide whether you really want this new role. It is vital that you consider your long-term goals and whether you will be happy to lead a group of people. Money should not be your key deciding criteria because it is the consequence of being excellent at what you do!

Assuming you decide to go for the sales leadership position, you will have opened up a series of opportunities and challenges. How you take them will decide your chances of success and growth.

Your biggest challenge

Your biggest challenge here is to transition yourself

from your earlier position as a salesperson to this new role where you lead a team. The skills and actions that helped you become a successful salesperson may not help you become an excellent leader. This is where you must "unlearn" some of your skills that no longer support your new role and "learn" new skills that will help you thrive.

For example, you were responsible for a big client doing all the work to win business, and now, as a leader, you delegate this account to your subordinate. This means that you let them take the lead, undertake the tasks you were doing before, and be the focal point for this client. You are no longer the salesperson but a leader who has people reporting to you who want to shine and want to be bankable. For many leaders, this can be nerve-racking!

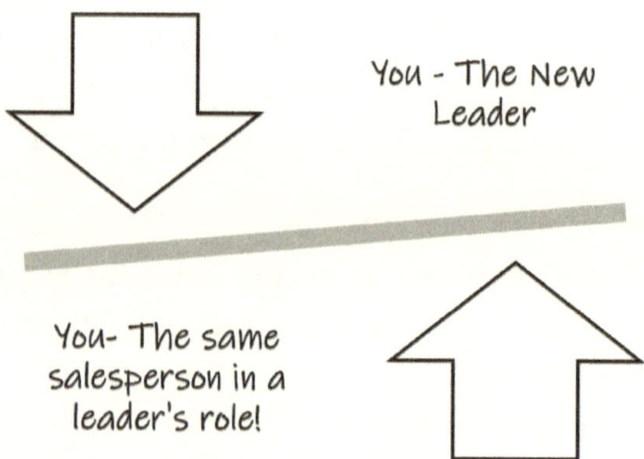

Knowing that you don't have all the skills for this new role requires some humility and the ability to think about yourself objectively. Knowing that some other leader or colleague in your team has a quality that you can learn from and approaching them to do just that also requires a desire to get better at what you do. If you have been doing great at sales, meeting lots of clients, and seeking their feedback, the chances are you have enough humility and collaboration skills that will be helpful to you during this transition.

Legacy

After you have understood your main challenge and transitioned into your leadership role, it is time to decide what your legacy would be.

Is it not too soon?

No!

Focusing on how you will be remembered after you get a further promotion or quit the job can be instrumental in setting your priorities right from the beginning. This will also nudge you to see things objectively and use a growth mindset to expand your comfort zones or completely get out of the comfort zones. You will automatically start getting into the habit of long-term thinking and doing things that matter most for which you were hired in the first place.

Maybe, you want to spend the rest of your career in this new leadership role, or maybe, you aspire to be the CEO of your company. Or you may want to use this experience to start a new business or a non-profit. The areas you focus on in this role will decide whether you achieve your goals.

Since you have people reporting to you, this is a chance for you to shape their lives for the better.

How do you decide which factors to focus on? What if these focus areas don't bring the desired results?

There are three main actions that will decide how you will perform at your job and how you will be remembered after you have moved on to some other role in the future-

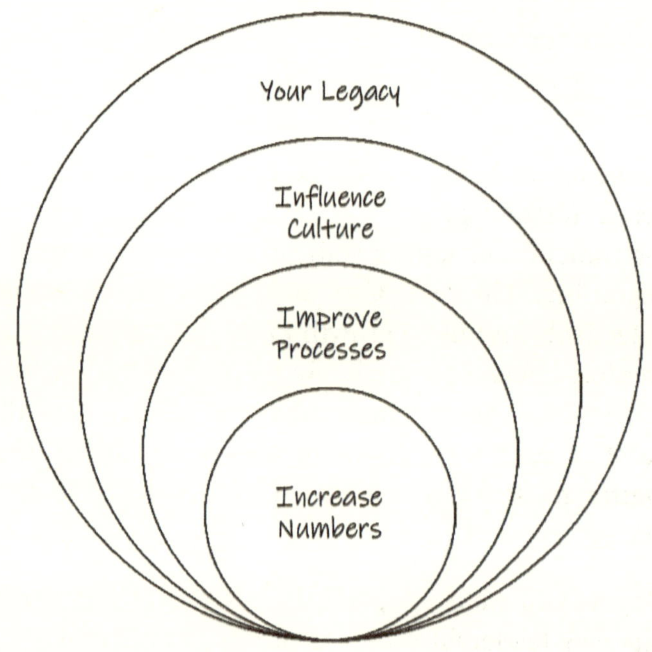

How you make better sales, improve the processes, and influence the working culture in this role will determine what legacy you leave behind.

<u>QUESTIONS FOR LEARNING</u>

1. As a sales leader, what is expected of me?
2. If I quit my job today, what are the top 2-3 things for which I will be remembered?
3. What are the most obvious things that need to change? How do I be the catalyst for this change?

<u>*NEXT STEP*</u>

The next three chapters are devoted to learning how you, as a sales leader, could increase numbers, improve processes, and influence the culture in your group and company.

16

Numbers

This is so obvious, so why discuss it? Well, all actions don't lead to the desired results, and hence, it is critical to decide key areas for action, which will help you, along with your team, grow the business.

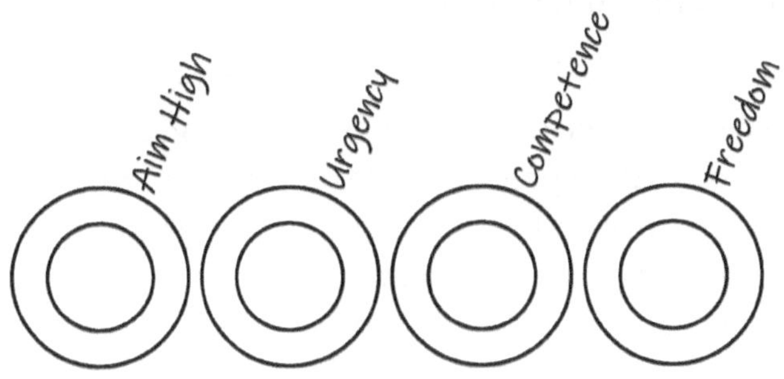

1. Set the bar "realistically" high!

The team cannot perform better than the bar their leader sets! If the expectations are too low, mediocrity and sloppy thinking set in, which can kill the business quickly. If the targets are unrealistic, your team will not achieve them. You must use your experience to see which business areas or products can do better in the market.

Once you zero in on them, be bold enough to set the target to focus on these areas. Do it a few times, and your team will start to stretch themselves to achieve more. This is natural, and all you need are some ambitious goals and close follow-ups. Make sure that you distribute the work among your team equitably before you expect excellent results for each of your team members.

Apart from meeting order intake goals, focus on profitability. Your salespeople must sell products at profit levels that can sustain your company. If your company makes excellent products but cannot sell at sustainable profits, you probably don't have the right sales team and the sales leader, i.e., you!

Cost-cutting is another way to improve profits. The problem is you cannot cut costs beyond a specific limit, and the chances are, you will demotivate the team. So focus on selling more and at higher profits. This way, you give a clear message that you are a growth-oriented leader rather than the penny-pinching type.

A leader like you, who sets high expectations and has excellent delegation skills, is what your team needs to do better than they think they can do.

Customers don't like to be sold but would like to be guided to buy your products. Apart from your products and services, your customers are looking for a great experience during the sales process and satisfaction after they use your product and services. Make sure that your sales team understand this and use it every day.

Moreover, this is a logical argument to not have "sales" in the title for your salespeople. They could be called "Business Development Managers" or something else that is subtler yet achieves the same goal, i.e., selling.

2. Instill a sense of urgency

This is a direct consequence of setting the bar high and a pre-requisite to meet the expectations.

If your salespeople are attending lots of internal meetings and sitting in front of their computers most of the time, you must question what is stopping them from visiting the clients.

How many customer problems are your team handling that are urgent? Are they able to find the right problems that need to be solved, bringing in more business? Do your salespeople know where they are traveling next week or the week after?

One of the benchmarks to understand whether there is a sense of urgency in your team is to see how many of them push you for answers. For example, suppose there is a tender with a deadline for which they need your help to allocate resources and get the pricing. Are they waiting for you to ask them? How proactive are they in approaching you for support? These are small things, but they go a long way to knowing if your people are on their toes or just relaxing.

If one or more of your team rarely comes to you with pressing problems that need quick action, you need to question their engagement at work and willingness to handle difficult tasks.

3. Match capabilities with tasks

Competence is the key to bringing great results.

Delegating your tasks to subordinates is now a part of your new role. It is time to assess if the person is capable of excelling in the tasks that you delegate. It is not good enough to be OK!

For example, you were handling some customers as a salesperson, and now your subordinate must take over your role. Since you have been excellent in your job all along, your customer has been getting world-class service from you, raising their expectations. Is your replacement capable of continuing this legacy? No two people are the same, but your customer has been used to excellent service from you and your company. Just because there is a new person in your role does not mean client expectations will be any lower!

Sometimes, you will join a new company in a sales leadership position and inherit the team from your predecessor. Spend a lot of time talking to them to understand what they believe are the strengths and weaknesses of your products and the team. When you identify the improvement area, make sure you change things and let them know why you are doing them.

Since you are new to the role, they are also trying to "figure you out" and "what are you up to." So don't change things too quickly unless you conclude that you have inherited an incompetent team. Find out how to cover their "manageable" weaknesses with a combination of feedback, delegation, training, and empowerment.

You will spend a lot of time with your team, and your chances of success depend on how they perform. Be sure that you have the right team.

4. Freedom

It is not enough to expect more from your team and delegate with a clear deadline. Do you provide enough freedom for your sales team to operate?

For example, your sales rep has been invited for a critical meeting and presentation by a reputed client. What do you do?

A. Ask them to prepare slides, and you deliver the presentation! Is that the most optimum?
B. Ask them to prepare the slides and let them deliver the presentation with you also joining for the meeting. You answer most of the

      questions asked by clients with your sales rep just standing by and looking awkward!

C. Let them attend the meeting and do all the necessary preparation. You guide them only if asked. All you do is seek feedback after they are back from the meeting and agree on the next steps.

If you have been doing the first two things, you are simply a bottleneck for your team achieving any success.

To be a great leader, you must trust your people, and they will bring out the best in themselves. This will also be reflected in the revenue and profits your team will achieve.

You must overcome your most significant challenge we discussed at the beginning of this chapter, i.e., doing things that your new leadership role demands and doing less of your salesperson role, which you have been used to doing for the most part of your career!

If you do these four things well, your business will grow, and that will make you more valuable in your company.

Your team will also look at you as their ambassador for their success and engagement at work.

They will respect you for what you do for them, and there is a good chance that they will be loyal to you and your company for a long time.

It's a win-win!

QUESTIONS FOR LEARNING

1. What is the maximum achievable target I should set up for the team?
2. Do I see a sense of urgency in my team to exceed the target? If not, how do I address it?
3. How do I ensure the expectations I have set for my team match their capabilities? Which areas do I need to tweak?
4. Am I allowing the necessary freedom to my team members, so they do their tasks effectively with minimum supervision? How could I improve on this?

NEXT STEP

As you improve the numbers, your influence within your company starts to increase. This gives you a chance to make processes better. Read the next chapter to find out more.

17

Processes

Processes are agreed ways of doing things within a company. Businesses need processes to run effectively. Without efficient processes, the chances of success are very dim.

Whether well-defined or not, your team also operates using some conventional ways of doing things.

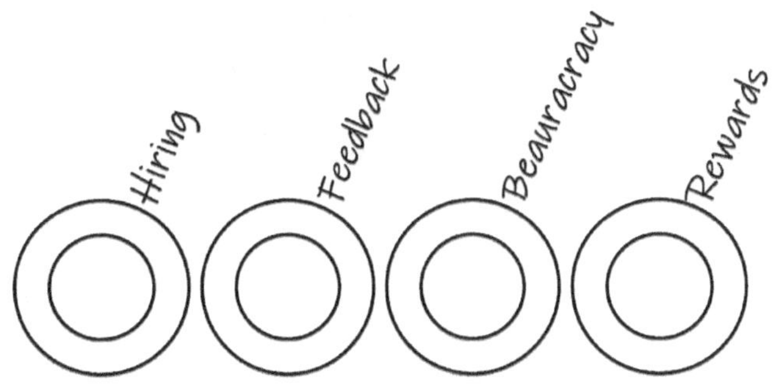

1. Hiring

Recruitment must be an area of core-competency for any leader, or any company for that matter.

Collective wisdom suggests that you should hire people that have the right competencies to bring results and have the integrity to align with company values.

Since you will spend a lot of time with your team and rely on them to achieve the results (including your yearly bonus), you must be excellent at hiring.

Before you interview the candidates, ask yourself-

- Why should this candidate join me rather than my competitor?
- Which interesting and challenging problems will they help solve for the company that will motivate the candidate to accept the offer?
- Will the candidate fit into the team?

Since you cannot be good at everything and cannot do all business tasks by yourself (you shouldn't, anyway), hire people who could compensate for your weaknesses. Your team members should have diverse skills that will make the team efficient and dynamic. Do not outsource hiring or trust headhunters.

Hire the right people of different nationalities and

with diverse backgrounds. Make sure that there is adequate gender diversity in your team without sacrificing meritocracy. This can help you seek multiple perspectives when you are seeking solutions to customer problems.

Look for people who are good listeners and have an outward focus (focus on the customers) rather than inward focus (focus on office, systems, tools, meetings, etc.).

When you hire experienced people, make sure that they integrate into your company culture and the team quickly. A new hire needs to assure themselves that your existing team has accepted them as a member, and they have made the right decision to quit their previous job.

Sometimes, you will hire salespeople from your competitors. The benefit is that they can start producing results quickly because they know the products and the customers. Your training costs can be meager. But have you thought about why they want to join you? If money is their primary goal, think twice before hiring them. The person who can switch loyalty just for money once can do it again. Make sure that they have the right reasons to quit their job and join you!

After you hire great talent, make sure that you retain them. Most companies say that they are equal opportunity employers. Do they practice what they say? Generally, people want to do a good job and want career growth. They want to have a good working atmosphere where their talent can be seen and appreciated. They want to feel that they are working for a goal or cause. Continually exchanging ideas with your subordinates and implementing some good ones will show them that you value them. Trust, equality, and genuine appreciation can help you retain good people. Simple things like letting people work from home 1-2 days a week can go a long way in showing that you trust them. Surprisingly, money is not the most important factor in talent retention.

That brings us to the unpleasant task of firing people. Sometimes, the market situation or your company's financial situation will require that you let go of some people. Do that with empathy and make sure to pay all their money. Write a good recommendation letter that could be valuable for them to get a new job.

You also might have to fire people if they are incompetent or lack teamwork, even if your company and the markets are doing well. In this case, make sure you explain the decision to the other team members so they don't start feeling insecure in the job. This is also a message to them to bring more business and become a proactive part of the team. This is part of your job as a leader.

Never forget to show empathy and professionalism to the person being laid off.

2. Feedback

In business, you will win some and lose some. The idea is to learn from your mistakes and not repeat them. Also, to learn from your success stories and make use of them in other areas.

Nothing beats having a great feedback mechanism in achieving both these goals. You must encourage a habit of asking for and giving feedback if it improves business, even if no one is asking. This also means that you and your team members must improve listening skills, which is one of the foundations of an effective feedback mechanism.

For example, your sales rep was working very hard on getting a deal, but the customer decided to choose your competitor. What do you do?

    A. Yell at them for losing! This won't work for anyone's benefit.

    B. Give an example of another team member who brings more business and advise that they should learn from them. This would not motivate them, either.

    C. Sit down with them and ask what they could do differently next time, so you win? What additional support they need from you next time? Was your value proposition correct?

Did your team understand the problem and present the solution effectively?

Having a conversation with a genuine understanding that you want to help and not just find faults in others is essential. If you do it well and frequently, you will start gaining what many business leaders don't- respect from your team!

Make sure that you give positive feedback as frequently as you give negative feedback.

3. Bureaucracy

No matter how efficient you think your team has been, there is always a lot of bureaucracy.

For example, consider the procedures that are followed on how to approach resources in other departments, how to get approvals for critical decisions etc. The rationale behind setting up these procedures and processes must have been good, but the question is whether they are being used effectively.

Nothing saps motivation like bureaucracy. If your team member is required to take his great idea from one office to another and needs to convince dozens of people, you probably need to rethink how you could improve.

Try to segregate processes that bring business,

improve safety at work, and build teamwork from the ones that suck people's energy and time. Brainstorm with your team whether you need those time-wasting processes, and if the answer is no, kill them with immediate effect.

This brings us to the issue of empowerment. If every small decision needs to be vetted by the top management, you simply don't have an agile organization. This will show up in employee engagement at work and how profitable your business is.

In this leadership role, challenge some of the processes that are not effective, which could save you money in the long run if discarded.

4. Rewards Policy

Suppose you set big goals for your team, and they rise to the occasion! You have nailed it! They continue to succeed year after year, making you more and more successful in your career. How do you reward them for this excellent effort?

As companies have fewer and fewer hierarchies, the chances of getting regular promotions are getting fewer. With flat structures, the salary levels are also similar for people on the same level. So how do you reward your high performers?

You must find ways to address this matter. After all,

you need high performers in your team today, as well as tomorrow, to continue in your pursuit of bringing excellent results. One of the ways to tackle this is by asking whether some of your high achievers are interested in lateral career movement. This could mean taking over sales responsibility for a new region or new product or merely doing something completely different that is important for the growth of the company. This could also mean relocating to a foreign office to work in an entirely different market and culture.

If you have been working closely with your team, you will be able to find out what each of them is looking for to a reasonable extent. You may not be able to fulfill all the wishes of all of them, but the fact that you have a keen interest in their aspirations and are taking concrete actions will be productive in the longer run.

Pay attention to these four things and make changes if necessary. A leaner and more effective organization can create wonders!

QUESTIONS FOR LEARNING

1. What are the critical processes across the company that affect my work?
2. How do I hire and retain talent?
3. How do I embed an effective feedback mechanism in the team?
4. Which processes are too bureaucratic and don't produce desired results? How do I change or stop them?
5. How do I make sure that there is a fair reward policy in my team?
6. For the changes I need to make, who are the other stakeholders I need to convince? How do I do it, and what timeframe do I set?

NEXT STEP

Your team is bringing excellent results under your leadership. You have also improved many processes, which are showing results. This is the time for you to start improving your company culture. Do more of what works and challenge what does not work. Be bold!

18

Culture

The late, great management guru Peter Drucker famously said that "culture eats strategy for breakfast!" Setting ambitious targets and actions to grow business without getting the culture right is like trying to build a supercar with an unreliable engine. The engine will break down from time to time, and you will forget to enjoy the drive and the car.

You were an integral part of your company culture before you became a leader. But with the new role, you have a real chance to influence the culture. You have your team looking at you to bring something more to the table than your predecessor, and it is your responsibility to challenge others if you think a cultural shift is needed in your company. It is difficult to put this in your job description because the company culture represents every employee, irrespective of their influence in changing the culture if needed.

A company is a set of a few teams, and a team is a set of people who want to achieve some common goals. Company culture binds them like glue!

Here are some ways to know your company culture and what to do if it needs fixing!

1. Teamwork

Mutual respect, collaboration, and co-operation are the pillars of any good team. How do you find out the level of teamwork in your team?

For example, one of your subordinates wins a big order. Your team has been supporting them to present a great value proposition, and the efforts of the team have paid off. But you notice that your subordinate is taking credit for this win as if it is only because of them. This is not the sign of good teamwork. You must have a conversation with them to make sure that they understand and acknowledge the contribution of their colleagues in their success. Also, consider thanking all the team members for their contribution, so they know you have been watching.

There are other examples such as people making false expense statements or regularly taking sick leave without being sick. Whether they realize it or not, these habits spill over to the other members of your team, and before you know it, a culture is formed.

From time to time, remind your team that teamwork is the only way you can all achieve your goals. Convey through your actions that you won't tolerate lone wolves and that you value the teamwork very much.

2. Trust and Accountability

You must instill a clear sense of accountability in every team member.

As you are setting bigger goals for you and your team, your team members should also be able to rise to the occasion. The best way to convince them is to let them know in no uncertain terms that they are accountable for their actions.

This will give you freedom from a need to micromanage them. Your job is to look at the future from a higher vantage point, and your subordinates have been hired to support you to achieve the goals set for them.

If you don't hold them accountable for their job, there is a good possibility that you end up doing many things that they should be doing and don't do many of the tasks that you should be doing. This leads to a culture where people start questioning your role.

Trust them and hold your team members accountable for what they do. If done right, this will also motivate them to expand their capabilities.

3. Groupthink

Suppose you are holding a brainstorming session to find ways to improve the sales of a product that is exceptionally good but not producing the expected business. You ask your team members about where you are lagging. They hesitate to answer until you talk about a few areas for improvement. After this, they start speaking up, showing how much they agree with you.

If this happens frequently, you have a team that is afraid to speak out and worries about how you will take it! This is not a team that will challenge you, disagree with you, and bring new game-changing ideas.

This could also mean that you have not been giving them enough space to think differently (than you do) and share their ideas. Maybe you have been doing a lot of talking and very little listening. Over time, this team will lose their ability to think independently and bring great ideas to you. Don't let this happen!

As a leader, strive to create a culture where people express their views openly and others listen without interruption. Find people in your team who disagree with you and try to understand their rationale objectively. Don't be threatened by them because they have different opinions or better ideas than you, but rather, take them on board and implement some of their ideas if they help you improve business. This will improve teamwork and employee engagement and help you achieve your goals faster.

Often, when you see things with fresh eyes, some things seem so inefficient or foreign. You get told "that's how we do things here" – be very suspicious of that. Always be good at taking a step back, being an outsider from the inside. Always be open to different ways of doing things but remain objective.

When a company talks about innovating, they should be talking about empowering people to bring different ideas that could lead to innovation if implemented in time.

When you foster a culture of encouraging people to share different viewpoints and ideas, you take the company culture to a whole new level.

This could be your most significant influence on others as a leader. You will be remembered for this after you leave your current role.

Having a positive influence on the culture and optimizing processes will automatically improve your chances of getting more business.

Your coworkers will remember you for more good reasons than otherwise!

QUESTIONS FOR LEARNING

1. How do I improve teamwork to achieve the targets? How do I monitor that the level of teamwork is healthy?
2. How do I communicate that I trust my subordinates and hold them accountable for their actions (without scaring them!)?
3. How much independent thinking goes on in my team? How do I encourage them to voice their opinions freely?
4. How do I make sure that I implement those ideas that bring more business?

19

What We Learned?

Thank you for reading the book.

Next time you visit a prospect or an existing customer, you will focus on asking the right questions to start building your value proposition.

We began by asking ourselves whether we want to continue a career in sales. I believe this question gave you enough motivation to think hard about your career choice and act if you felt that this is not the right career for you.

We discussed business plans and how to focus on growth, i.e., making more sales year after year. Even while you are preparing a business plan, the process itself will make you think about many aspects of your job and understand what actions matter most and how they should be executed.

Talking about the execution of the business plan, we discussed why targets and goals should be realistic yet challenging. The actions that you decide to take to achieve your targets will be totally in line with your business plan. Hopefully, you embark on a habit of acting on things that help you achieve your goals and discard other actions that won't help you toward reaching your targets. As someone with a lot of integrity, you are now trusted with important assignments by your management. With time-management awareness, you are cutting down on time-wasting tasks. Your focus has improved, and that will bring amazing results.

After we set the foundation for being an effective salesperson, we discussed the value proposition. When you consciously develop an eye for finding the pain areas of your customers, it will take you closer to finding the right solutions for them and differentiate your solution from your competition. You will be able to solve customer problems in a better way than your competitors. Your killer presentations and listening skills will increase customer engagement during the meetings. Awareness of stakeholder mapping will nudge you to find the right people from the customer's side to conclude the sale faster.

We also looked at things from a buyer's perspective. While the buyer wants to commoditize, to drag the prices down, you now have enough firepower to switch the discussion to the value you bring.

Companies are not in the charity business, and neither are you! As you spend a significant part of your life working, it is important to also think about yourself. Whether it is vertical or lateral career growth, you are now aware of which factors affect your career and how to maneuver through them.

The result is more sales, more premiums, better career growth, and a job you love. That's a dream come true!

The last section of the book saw you taking up a sales leadership position and taking time to decide what your legacy would be after you move on. I hope you understand how privileged you are in this position as you can impact other people's lives. I am sure that you will increase the business, improve the processes, and influence your company culture in a positive way.

Your coworkers will remember you for more good reasons than otherwise!

Happy selling!

20

Using This Book

Congratulations! You have finished the book. What do you do now?

I hope that the book covered various aspects of sales and sales career. Questions at the end of each chapter made you think deeply about how you are selling, and which actions will help you sell more.

In this last chapter, start a habit of asking yourself some great questions that will help you become better at winning the game. Below are questions-

3 important questions I should answer to decide whether a sales career suits me?

____

____

____

3 important questions I should answer to understand what I have been hired to do?

---

3 important questions I should answer about my business plan?

---

3 important questions I should answer when deciding on goals and targets for the next three months?

---

3 important questions I should answer when deciding on actions to grow business every week?

---

3 important questions I should answer for better time management every day?

---

3 important questions I should answer to find the best value proposition in every potential sale?

____

____

____

3 important questions I should answer to make a killer presentation every single time?

____

____

____

3 important questions I should answer about stakeholders in every important meeting?

____

____

____

3 important questions I should answer about the buyer's needs and expectations in every sales process with each customer?

____

____

____

3 important questions I should answer about the price I am asking?

____

____

---

3 important questions I should answer before I go for any price negotiation with a customer?

---

3 important questions I should answer before I decide whether I want a sales leadership role?

---

3 important questions I should answer as a sales leader to decide what legacy I wish to leave behind?

---

3 important questions I should answer as a sales leader to decide how I could improve the business output and collaboration in my team?

---

3 important questions I should answer as a sales leader to decide which processes need to be improved to get better results?

____

____

____

3 important questions **I** should answer as a sales leader to decide which actions will positively influence the working culture?

____

____

____

Onward...

Bonus!

Don't forget yourself!

Be Famous!

Celebrities are in the business of being famous! Their career and bank balance depend a lot on how their audience perceives them. Everybody needs some publicity, including you!

As a salesperson, you meet different people and leave impressions. The problem here is that your area of influence is limited by the geography in which you operate. Thankfully, there is something magical called LinkedIn!

Whether you are starting your sales career or near retirement, LinkedIn is relevant for you and can create wonders if used properly. LinkedIn is a tool for professional networking with a human touch.

For example, if you sell technologies that help reduce carbon emissions, you are contributing something much more significant than you - the fight against climate change.

Below are the things you can do on LinkedIn to gain more knowledge in tackling the issue-

- Connect with people in a similar industry
- Find companies who are also contributing
- Find new ideas that help you learn more
- Share your ideas that help others learn more
- Ask a question and get some professional advice
- Form a community to continue your journey

All you need is a mobile or PC with an internet connection. Well, you need a little more than that, which we will discuss now!

Here are some essential things you could do to improve your visibility and contribute to the business area you belong to or any other meaningful activity you wish to undertake-

Your Profile Photo

Since it is all about you, your profile photo should look the best version of who you are! This is not the place to show your vacation or family photo, but rather, it should be a professional-looking photo. It should convey that you value yourself and have spent the time to take a good photo.

Your Headline

This is the place to showcase what you can do for

others that will make you valuable to them. It could be problems you can solve, consulting you can do, or just sell them something they need.

You could also write your title like Account Manager, followed by your area of business, such as environmental sustainability.

Don't write what you are not!

Who are you?

The next important thing is a summary of your work experience. The idea is to write which industry you belong to and what problems you can solve for others. This is the place to write enough words about yourself that will help you get noticed by others. If a potential customer visits your account and sees a professional photo and a relevant headline, they will go through your experience and might want to approach you to solve some problems for them. You have just created a new business opportunity that could help you and your prospect. All for free!

Experience and Education

You write about your employment history and education. Keep this short and simple so others can quickly understand. Don't lie about your accomplishments or qualifications or take credit for other people's work.

Add Skills

You can add skills that you think you are good at, and ones that could bring some value to someone else. Be realistic! For example, if you have two months of experience as a salesperson, don't write leadership and mentoring as your skills.

Endorsements & Recommendations

Unlike the skills that you write yourself, you cannot write your own endorsement and recommendation! If your client is happy about something you did for them, ask for an endorsement. This way, other clients will see that you have helped this client and will want to know more. Maybe they are facing a problem that you have already solved, and before you know it, this prospect is hooked!

Interests

This is the place of great potential for free learning! Try to follow some key companies and people in your industry and read their posts often. In a year or two, you will have gained a lot more knowledge from this community.

If you are fantastic at something, focus on it and keep posting, and very soon, others will start following you.

Many times, others will post some questions, and if

you happen to have a great answer, just write it.

Congratulations- you are on your way to becoming an "influencer!" You could end up doing TED Talks!

Your connections

LinkedIn uses an algorithm, which means it shows you more of what it thinks you are! If you are not mindful of your profile and posts, you might end up having a network that is not relevant. Every time you get a new connection request, think about the relevance before you accept it. For example, suppose you just attended an exhibition where you showcased your products. You had many visitors, including people who don't belong to your industry. If you accept their connection request, you start belonging to other industries on LinkedIn, which is counterproductive. So, if you sell engineering products, don't get connected with car rental companies or flower sellers! You might just become one in the LinkedIn database!

Don't be in the race to have connections, but rather, find at least 500+ relevant connections that will give you a solid base. When you meet exciting clients, try to connect with them after the meeting. As you start posting interesting things that are useful for them, they will start following you, and a bond is created. You have just made yourself accessible to them whenever they need you!

Your company

If you own a business, LinkedIn is a great tool to connect with your prospects. If you work for a company, you could help your company get noticed among prospective clients. If your company does not have an active LinkedIn promotion policy, you must encourage them to get on board!

If you want to check out my LinkedIn profile, here is the link-

https://www.linkedin.com/in/prad1979

Is it the ONLY tool? No!

Below are some other ideas that could make you famous-

- Become an authority in your area and make presentations at prestigious conferences.
- Join groups of similar people in your profession and develop contacts.
- Publish papers or write articles in business magazines.
- Make videos that help customers solve some problems and post them on YouTube.
- Publish a book!

Acknowledgments

I thank all those who believed in this book from the start.

Special thanks to my wife, kids, and my parents for encouraging me to finish this book.

Thanks to my colleagues and friends who gave their honest feedback and improvement ideas during the writing of this book.

Thanks to the folks at Happy Self Publishing for their services and guidance.

Special thanks to Amazon for providing such an easy and excellent platform for people like me to share their ideas with the world.

I hope that my effort will inspire others to unleash their creativity.

About the Author

Prashant Dongre has been working in sales & business development for the past 20 years, mainly in the oil and gas industry. He has traveled to and served customers in more than 15 countries. He considers himself lucky to have been given excellent opportunities by his past and current employers and managers to help customers.

He lives in the Middle East with his wife and three kids.

He can be contacted on iprad21@gmail.com

Or https://www.linkedin.com/in/prad1979
Or at www.b2bsteps.com

Thank You

Thank You for Reading My Book!

I really appreciate all of your feedback, and I love hearing what you have to say.

I need your input to make the next version of this book and my future books even better.

Please leave me a helpful review on Amazon letting me know what you thought of the book.

Thank you so much!
Prashant Dongre

www.ingramcontent.com/pod-product-compliance
Lightning Source LLC
Chambersburg PA
CBHW031037160726
47991CB00005B/1920